PSYCHOLOGICAL TESTING
History, Principles, and Applications

Instructor's Manual and Test Bank
for

PSYCHOLOGICAL TESTING
History, Principles, and Applications

SECOND EDITION

Robert J. Gregory
Wheaton College

Allyn and Bacon
Boston · London · Toronto · Sydney · Tokyo · Singapore

TABLE OF CONTENTS

PREFACE

This manual is designed as a companion to the textbook, *Psychological Testing: History, Principles, and Applications* (2nd Ed.) by Robert J. Gregory. The 30 topics in this manual correspond to each of the 30 topics in the textbook. For each topic, the instructor will find the following:

Classroom Discussion Questions

Extramural Assignments

Classroom Demonstrations

Essay Questions

Test Item File

This manual serves two purposes. First, the instructor will find numerous and diverse approaches to improving the quality of a course on psychological testing. For example, the classroom discussion questions will encourage students to think about difficult and controversial issues in psychological testing. The classroom demonstrations are designed to liven up the class periods. Also, the extramural assignments will help broaden the students' grasp of psychological and psychometric concepts.

The second purpose of the manual is to provide the instructor with ready-made multiple choice and essay questions. In all, the manual incorporates more than 1,000 multiple choice questions, plus dozens of suggested essay questions. Every single question was written by the author, so the textbook intentions are well represented in the pedagogy of this manual.

Teaching is a complex and demanding task. I hope that the modest resources provided here will help the instructor with this difficult but rewarding endeavor.

Robert J. Gregory

Topic 1A

The Origins of Psychological Testing

The Importance of Testing

Case Exhibit 1.1: The Consequences of Test Results

Rudimentary Forms of Testing in China in 2200 B.C.

Psychiatric Antecedents of Psychological Testing

The Brass Instruments Era of Testing

    Galton and the First Battery of Mental Tests
    Cattell Imports Brass Instruments to the U.S.

Changing Conceptions of Mental Retardation in the 1800s
    Esquirol and Diagnosis in Mental Retardation
    Seguin and Education of the Mentally Retarded

Influence of Binet's Early Research Upon His Test

Binet and Testing for Higher Mental Processes

Summary

Classroom Discussion Questions

1. Students are so accustomed to the idea of psychological testing that they rarely consider the consequences of this practice. A good starting point for a class on psychological testing is to ask students to provide anecdotal reports about the consequences of psychological testing. Almost everyone can provide an anecdote about themselves or someone they know well. The crucial question to ask is: How might your life (or that of your acquaintance) be different if the results of the testing had been better or worse? What decisions were predicated upon the results?

2. A related question pertains to the original application of intelligence tests. Binet and Simon were asked to fashion a test to identify children who would not profit from ordinary schooling. It is interesting to ask students whether they believe this use of psychological testing is constructive or not. Such a discussion will get them thinking about the extra-validity concerns encountered later in the book.

3. The concept of IQ is introduced at the end of Topic 1A. Overall, how do students feel about the concept of IQ? What is their understanding of it? Remember that the original Binet-Simon scale did not make reference to an IQ or a score, but was used in an impressionistic manner. Could we get along without scores in the modern American school system?

Extramural Assignments

1. If your students have access to the *Journal of the History of the Behavioral Sciences*, ask them to find and summarize a few articles on the early history of psychological testing. They might be surprised to discover the level of sophistication that early test developers incorporated into their endeavors.

2. Challenge the students to develop their own version of the 1905 Binet-Simon Scale and administer it to a sample of young and old children. For example, the scale might consist of 10 to 20 items similar to those depicted in Table 1.1. The students could administer

the test to samples of children ages 2, 4, and 8 to observe how item pass rates increase with age.

Classroom Demonstrations

1. An interesting project would be to investigate the relationship between modern cognitive measures of intelligence and measures akin to Galton and Cattell's "brass instruments." In the simplest possible design, students could take a short cognitive measure (e.g., Shipley Institute of Living Scale) and also assess their reaction time via computer or other approach. A scatterplot of scores and Pearson r could be used to determine whether these two approaches have any relationship. It would be useful to discuss such issues as reliability of measurement (are the RTs reliable?) and restriction of range (would the results differ if students from a wider range of abilities were used?).

2. Francis Galton was so important in the history of psychological testing that the instructor may find it useful to prepare a short talk on this fascinating genius. The biography of Galton by Pearson (1914, 1924, 1930a,b) contains a wealth of detail about Galton and his views. Boring (1950) devotes a short section to Galton's contributions as well.

3. Wissler's (1901) article is usually available in most libraries or can be acquired by inter-library loan. Since it marked the end of the brass instruments era of testing, students may enjoy a more detailed presentation of this piece of seminal research.

Essay Questions

1. In one or two short sentences, describe the most important contributions to psychological testing of the following persons: Wilhelm Wundt, Francis Galton, J. McK. Cattell, Clark Wissler, Alfred Binet.

2. Discuss how the IQ concept was invented and speculate upon the positive and negative consequences of this concept.

TEST ITEM FILE

Topic 1: Origins of Psychological Testing

1.   Who is generally credited with developing the first battery of psychological tests?
     a. J. McKeen Cattell
     b. Alfred Binet
     c. Henry Goddard
   *d. Francis Galton

2.   The psychologist who set the modern agenda for psychological testing by proclaiming "perhaps" tests would be useful in "training, mode of life or indication of disease" was
   *a. J. McKeen Cattell
     b. Alfred Binet
     c. Henry Goddard
     d. Francis Galton

3.   Regarding the impact of psychological testing, the text takes the position that tests
     a. typically certify what is already known about persons
     b. perform a mainly ceremonial or symbolic role
   *c. commonly alter individual destiny in profound ways
     d. all of the above

4.   Historical developments are pertinent to contemporary testing for the following reasons:
     a. they help explain current practices that might otherwise seem arbitrary or even peculiar
     b. the strengths and limitations of testing stand out better when tests are viewed in historical context
     c. history helps remind us not to be overly zealous in our modern-day applications of testing
   *d. all of the above

5. The first applications of testing can be traced to
   *a. Chinese testing of officials for office in 2200 B.C.
   b. Galton's sensory tests in the late 1800s
   c. Wissler's 1901 correlation of tests and academic marks
   d. Binet's 1905 testing of Paris school children

6. Civil service examinations were first introduced in
   a. the United States
   b. France
   c. Great Britain
   *d. China

7. In early Chinese testing, the beauty of penmanship was weighted very heavily in determining test scores. Why?
   a. because of cultural norms that emphasized esthetics
   *b. good penmanship was essential to fitness for office
   c. one early emperor had an obsession with appearances
   d. the reason is completely unknown, lost in history

8. Five subjects (civil law, military affairs, agriculture, revenue, and geography) were tested in this country's civil service examination.
   a. the United States
   b. France
   c. Great Britain
   *d. China

9. The first memory drum was developed in _____ in about ____.
   a. the United States, 1805
   b. the United States, 1885
   c. Germany, 1805
   *d. Germany, 1885

10. In early psychiatric testing, many _____ patients could recognize stimuli in their totality but could not identify them when shown through a moving slot.
    *a. brain-injured
    b. schizophrenic
    c. mentally retarded
    d. manic-depressive

11. A test battery developed in 1889 by Rieger was impractical because
    a. the equipment kept breaking down
    b. the methods were vague and subjective
    c. many of the stimuli were painful
    *d. it took over 100 hours to administer

12. The "brass instruments" era was a deadend because
    *a. psychologists mistook simple sensory processes for intelligence
    b. the tests had a "ceiling" effect
    c. the tests had a "floor" effect
    d. there was no attempt to standardize testing methods

13. The "thought meter" was developed by
    a. Galton
    b. McK. Cattell
    *c. Wundt
    d. Schlosberg

14. The purpose of the "thought meter" was to
    a. test sensory acuity
    *b. measure the essential speed of thought
    c. prove the existence of imageless thoughts
    d. measure intelligence

15. Experiments with the "thought meter" were relevant to what well-known historical controversy?
    a. the existence of imageless thought
    b. the primacy of sensation over perception
    *c. individual differences in stellar crossing times
    d. the existence of instantaneous thought

16. Sir Francis Galton attempted to measure all of the following EXCEPT
    a. personality
    b. the boringness of lectures
    c. the efficacy of prayer
    *d. infant intelligence

17. Galton's methods were an improvement upon existing "brass instruments" approaches because they
    *a. allowed for quick and efficient data collection
    b. employed better indices of problem solving
    c. measured intelligence, not sensory acuity
    d. were highly reliable

18. To further his study of individual differences, Galton set up a psychometric laboratory at
    a. Wundt's laboratory in Leipzig, Germany
    b. Columbia University
    *c. the International Health Exhibition in London
    d. the Sorbonne in France

19. Regarding payment, what arrangement did Galton make with his subjects?
    a. he paid his subjects a small fee for participation
    *b. his subjects paid him a small fee to be tested
    c. testing was free
    d. subjects could donate money to the laboratory

20. Galton's test battery assessed all of the following EXCEPT
    a. head length
    b. strength of hand squeeze
    c. visual acuity
    *d. problem solving

21. J. McK. Cattell studied psychology with
    a. Binet
    b. Galton
    c. Wundt
    *d. both Galton and Wundt

22. Cattell's test battery was mainly an extension of the battery developed by
    *a. Galton
    b. Wundt
    c. Binet
    d. Wissler

23. The term "mental test" was first popularized by
    a. Galton
    *b. Cattell
    c. Binet
    d. Terman

24. Regarding the relationship between bodily energy and mental energy, Cattell believed
    a. there was no connection between the two
    b. mental energy determined bodily energy
    *c. the two were inseparable from one another
    d. bodily energy determined mental energy

25. All of the following persons studied under Cattell EXCEPT
    a. Thorndike
    b. Wissler
    c. Strong
    *d. Goddard

26. Whose results showed virtually no tendency for mental test scores to correlate with academic achievement?
    a. Thorndike
    *b. Wissler
    c. Strong
    d. Goddard

27. The path-breaking discovery that mental test scores do not correlate with academic achievement was published in
    a. 1879   c. 1917
    *b. 1901   d. 1933

28. By using only bright college students as subjects, early researchers inadvertently introduced a _____ which would invariably reduce the size of his correlations.
    a. cultural bias
    b. ceiling effect
    *c. restriction of range
    d. statistical artifact

29. Correlations of _____ between reaction time and intelligence are not at all uncommon.
    *a. -.40
    b. -.60
    c. .40
    d. .60

30. In measuring reaction time, Galton and others failed to obtain reliable measures because
    a. their equipment lacked sophistication
    b. they did not comprehend the nature of reaction time
    c. they assessed only visual reaction time
    *d. they used too few trials

31. A new humanism toward mentally retarded persons first arose in the
    a. 1600s
    b. 1700s
    *c. 1800s
    d. 1990s

32. The first true intelligence tests were developed for what purpose?
    a. to identify persons with superior intellect
    b. to test a complex theory on the growth and change of intellect in early childhood
    *c. to identify children who were unlikely to profit from ordinary instruction
    d. to solve a personal dispute between two of the most famous psychologists in history

33. The first person to write about the difference between mental illness and mental retardation was
    a. Seguin
    b. Binet
    c. Freud
    *d. Esquirol

34. The first person to propose a classification system for mental retardation was
    a. Seguin
    b. Binet
    c. Freud
    *d. Esquirol

35. The first classification system for mental retardation relied mainly upon
    a. problem solving abilities
    b. physical stigmata
    c. head circumference
    *d. language skills

36. The psychologist who devoted his life to developing educational programs for the retarded was
    *a. Seguin
    b. Binet
    c. Freud
    d. Esquirol

37. *Idiocy, and Its Treatment by the Physiological Method* was first published in _____ by _____
    a. 1786, Seguin
    *b. 1886, Seguin
    c. 1786, Binet
    d. 1886, Binet

38. The first modern intelligence test was invented in _____ by
    a. 1805, Cattell
    b. 1905, Cattell
    c. 1805, Binet
    *d. 1905, Binet

39. Binet began his career in psychology by studying the
    *a. two-point threshold
    b. intelligence of infants
    c. hypnotic treatment of hysteria
    d. method of free association

40. For a brief time, Binet's professional path paralleled that of
    a. Cattell
    b. Galton
  *c. Freud
    d. Jung

41. In response to public criticism, Binet recanted his early findings about   a. intelligence in newborns
  *b. magnetic induction of mood changes
    c. intelligence in mentally retarded persons
    d. calibration of the two-point threshold

42. From studies of _____ Binet concluded that attention was a key component of intelligence.
    a. problem solving in retarded adults
    b. reaction time in superior adults
    c. problem solving in children
  *d. reaction time in children

43. In the testing of children, Binet advocated
    a. strict experimental consistency
  *b. restarting procedures 10, 20 times, if necessary
    c. developing rapport before using specific procedures
    d. skepticism about positive results

44. In testing children, Binet warned psychologists to be on the lookout for   a. oppositional behavior
    b. suggestibility
    c. failure of attention
  *d. both suggestibility and failure of attention

45. The idea that intelligence could be better measured by means of the higher psychological processes rather than the elementary sensory processes such as reaction time was suggested in _____ in a paper by
  *a. 1896, Binet and Henri
    b. 1905, Binet and Henri
    c. 1896, Binet and Simon
    d. 1905, Binet and Simon

46. The character of the 1905 Binet and Simon scale owed much to a prior scale developed by
   a. Cattell
   b. Galton
   c. Sequin
   *d. Damaye

47. What was the advantage of the 1905 Binet and Simon scale over previous efforts?
   a. it was brief and practical
   b. it assessed practical judgment
   c. the items were arranged in order of difficulty
   *d. all of the above

48. Binet and Simon defined intelligence as the ability to
   a. adapt to the environment
   *b. judge well, understand well, and reason well
   c. solve abstract problems
   d. alternate quickly between the abstract and the concrete

49. The 1905 Binet and Simon scale was calibrated to a population average of
   a. 50
   b. 100
   c. 150
   *d. none of the above

50. The 1908 revision of the Binet and Simon scale included the following innovation(s):
   a. introduction of the IQ concept
   b. classification of levels of intelligence
   *c. introduction of the concept of mental level
   d. all of the above

51. The concept of "intelligence quotient" was suggested by _____ in _____.
   a. Galton, 1884
   *b. Binet, 1905
   c. Stern, 1912
   d. Terman, 1916

Topic 1B

Early Testing in the United States

Early Uses and Abuses of Tests in America

> First Translation of the Binet-Simon Scale
> The Binet-Simon and Immigration

The Invention of Nonverbal Tests in the Early 1900s

The Stanford-Binet: The Early Mainstay of IQ

Group Tests and the Classification of WWI Army Recruits

> The Army Alpha and Beta Examinations
> The Army Tests and Ethnic Differences

Early Educational Testing

The Development of Aptitude Tests

Personality and Vocational Testing After WWI

The Origins of Projective Testing

The Development of Interest Inventories

Summary of Major Landmarks in the History of Testiing

Summary

Classroom Discussion Questions

1. Much of Topic 1B concerns the early use of psychological tests with immigrants who did not speak English. The instructor might find it interesting to ask students to discuss the characteristics of a fair test within this population. This will likely lead into a discussion of the purposes of testing, the meaning of a test to different populations, culture-reduced testing, etc. All these concepts are taken up later in the textbook.

Extramural Assignments

1. One emphasis of Topic 1B is the use of psychological tests for military screening. Students might be asked to interview older persons who were inducted during during wartime (WW I, WW II, Korea, Vietnam) to form an impression about psychological testing in the military, its nature and purposes, etc.

2. Topic 1B lists a number of early classic references in psychological testing. Although many libraries do not carry these early journals, with enough advance preparation students could request reprints of selected articles. A written critique or oral presentation on these classic papers would serve a useful educational purpose. The following sources, referenced in the textbook, are especially recommended: Goddard (1911, 1912), Knox (1914), Kohs (1920), Pyle (1913), Yerkes (1921), and Brigham (1923).

Classroom Demonstrations

1. If the instructor can obtain samples of outmoded tests, a useful classroom demonstration concerns the issue of culture-loading. In particular, students can be shown sample items from early tests and asked to identify which items are culturally loaded and why. Then, students can be asked the crucial question: other than your opinion, what proof could be offered that a certain item is culturally loaded? It is unlikely that students will offer useful approaches so early in the

course, but it is worth arousing their interest in this issue, since it reoccurs later in the text.

2. If the instructor can obtain a copy of the Yerkes (1921) monograph, it is just filled with examples of early precursors to modern intelligence tests. Students are generally amazed to discover that Wechsler purloined many performance items directly from the work of WW I psychologists.

Essay Questions

1. Trace the history of the use of individual intelligence tests for immigration decisions in the early 1900s.

2. Describe the Army Alpha and Beta tests and discuss their use in military screening.

TEST ITEM FILE

Topic 1B: Early Testing in the United States

1. The first translation of the Binet-Simon scales was completed in
_____ by _____.
    a. 1910, Terman
    b. 1930, Terman
    *c. 1910, Goddard
    d. 1930, Goddard

2. At the turn of the century, the following labels were used for diagnostic purposes in mental retardation:
    *a. idiot, imbecile, feeble-minded
    b. retarded, feeble-minded, borderline
    c. imbecile, feeble-minded, borderline
    d. severely retarded, mildly retarded, borderline

3. Goddard considered children who were _____ to be feeble-minded.
   a. below an IQ of 70
   b. incapable of self-care
   c. trainable but not educable
   *d. mentally four or more years behind

4. Regarding immigration and "feeblemindedness," which of the following statements characterizes national opinion in the early 1900s?
   a. the feebleminded reproduced at an alarming rate
   b. newer immigrants were mentally inferior to traditional immigrants
   c. immigration threatened the nation's overall biological fitness
   *d. all of the above

5. Initially, Goddard was _____ about the purported threat of feeble-mindedness posed by the immigrants.
   a. excitedly alarmed
   b. alarmed
   c. cautiously concerned
   *d. unconcerned

6. What was Goddard's position with respect to restrictions upon immigration?
   a. he led the movement to restrict immigration
   b. he proposed different quotas for different countries
   *c. he did not join the popular call for immigration restriction
   d. he favored a complete ban upon immigration

7. What was Goddard's position with respect to heredity and intelligence?
   a. he was a strict hereditarian who conceived of intelligence in simple-minded Mendelian terms
   b. he believed that much undesirable behavior was due to inherited mental deficiency
   c. he called for the colonization of the mentally defective
   *d. all of the above

8. In testing small samples of immigrants, Goddard concluded that about ____ percent of them were "feebleminded."
   a. 20
   b. 40
   c. 60
   *d. 80

9. Goddard's views on mental retardation can be characterized as
   a. simple and consistent
   b. simple and inconsistent
   c. complex and consistent
   *d. complex and inconsistent

10. What was the incentive for developing nonverbal intelligence tests in the early 1900s?
    a. to test non-English speaking subjects
    b. to test illiterate persons
    c. to test the speech and hearing handicapped
    *d. all of the above

11. One of the earliest performance measures, the _____ is still used today in the Halstead-Reitan neuropsychological battery.
    a. Knox puzzle
    b. Kohs block design
    c. Porteus mazes
    *d. Seguin form board

12. It is appropriate to characterize the first Stanford-Binet as a _____ of the Binet-Simon scales.
    a. total revision
    *b. substantial revision
    c. slight revision
    d. faithful, literal translation

13. The first Stanford-Binet was useful mainly with
    a. mentally retarded persons
    b. normal and superior children
    c. normal and superior adults
    *d. all of the above

14. The latest revision of the Stanford-Binet was completed in
    a. 1916
    b. 1937
    c. 1960
    *d. 1986

15. The WWI effort to test army recruits was headed up by
    a. Goddard
    b. Terman
    *c. Yerkes
    d. Cattell

16. Two tests were used to test army recruits during WWI:
    *a. Alpha and Beta
    b. Alpha and Stanford-Binet
    c. Beta and Stanford-Binet
    d. Wechsler and Stanford-Binet

17. A nonverbal group test designed for use with illiterates and recruits whose first language was not English:
    a. Alpha
    *b. Beta
    c. Stanford-Binet
    d. Personal Data Sheet

18. A group test that consisted of eight verbally-loaded tests for average and high functioning recruits.
    *a. Alpha
    b. Beta
    c. Stanford-Binet
    d. Personal Data Sheet

19. The instructions on this test mainly used pictorial and gestural methods for explaining the questions and problems:
    a. Alpha
    *b. Beta
    c. Stanford-Binet
    d. Personal Data Sheet

20. Of what value was the WWI testing to the Army?
  *a. it is not really clear whether the Army made much use of the test results
  b. the Army used the test results to dramatically increase its efficiency
  c. the Army brass accepted the validity of the tests but opted for limited application
  d. the Army brass doubted the validity of the tests but based important decisions upon them anyway

21. Tens of thousands of WWI recruits received a literal zero for many Army subtests, because
  a. they were retarded
  *b. they didn't understand the instructions
  c. the tests were scored incorrectly
  d. instructors only pretended to give the tests

22. Regarding racial and ethnic differences in test scores, what was the outcome of the Army testing during WWI?
  a. the Army did not permit researchers to make racial and/or ethnic comparisons
  b. researchers made racial and ethnic comparisons and found no differences
  *c. test results were sometimes used to "substantiate" prejudices about various racial and ethnic groups
  d. the tests were only given to white subjects, so racial and ethnic comparisons were not possible

23. Who wrote "The process of racial intermixture cannot result in anything but an average of these elements, with the resulting deterioration of American intelligence"?
  a. Goddard
  b. Terman
  c. Yerkes
  *d. Brigham

24. Which researchers renounced their earlier views about the menace posed by "inferior" immigrants?
   a. Terman and Goddard
   *b. Goddard and Brigham
   c. Goddard and Pyle
   d. Terman and Brigham

25. Currently, most college admissions tests are directed by the
   a. College Entrance Examination Board
   b. Graduate Record Examination Board
   *c. Educational Testing Service
   d. College Admissions Board

26. A statistical technique known as _____ was needed for the development of sophisticated aptitude tests.
   *a. factor analysis
   b. multiple regression
   c. discriminant function analysis
   d. analysis of variance

27. Which psychologist believed that global measures of intelligence did not, so to speak, "cut nature at its joints"?
   a. Terman
   b. Yerkes
   *c. Thurstone
   d. Spearman

28. When the armed forces first started using specialized aptitude tests, washout rates:
   a. increased
   b. remained stable
   c. decreased slightly
   *d. decreased significantly

29. Modern personality testing began with the practical need to
   *a. identify WWI Army recruits susceptible to breakdown
   b. assess persons for employment suitability
   c. determine the emotional consequences of warfare
   d. classify WWII Army recruits for different positions

30. Virtually all modern personality tests owe a debt to the
   a. Minnesota Multiphasic Personality Inventory
   *b. Personal Data Sheet
   c. Bernreuter Personality Inventory
   d. Allport-Vernon Study of Values

31. The Thurstone Personality Schedule employed _____ in scale development.   a. empirical keying
                    b. factor analysis
                   *c. rational keying
                    d. psychoanalytic theory

32. One of the first personality tests to use the method of internal consistency in scale development was the
   a. Minnesota Multiphasic Personality Inventory
   b. Personal Data Sheet
   c. Bernreuter Personality Inventory
   *d. Thurstone Personality Schedule

33. One of the first personality tests to use the ipsative approach in scale development was the
   a. Minnesota Multiphasic Personality Inventory
   b. Personal Data Sheet
   c. Bernreuter Personality Inventory
   *d. Allport-Vernon Study of Values

34. The test that introduced the use of validity scales to determine fake bad, fake good, and random response patterns:
   *a. Minnesota Multiphasic Personality Inventory
   b. Personal Data Sheet
   c. Bernreuter Personality Inventory
   d. Allport-Vernon Study of Values

35. The researcher who gave himself four seconds to come up with as many associations as possible to a stimulus word was
   a. Jung
   b. Binet
   c. Kraepelin
   *d. Galton

36. Kent and Rosanoff (1910) gave the association method a distinctively American flavor by
     a. picking the stimulus words from a dictionary frequency count
     b. correlating responses with psychiatric diagnoses
    *c. tabulating the reactions of 1,000 normal subjects
     d. timing response latencies to the nearest tenth of a second

37. In developing his test, Rorschach was most heavily influenced by
     a. Freud
     b. Adler
    *c. Jung
     d. Galton

38. The hypothesis that we inadvertently disclose our inner-most needs, fantasies, and conflicts when responding to ambiguous or unstructured stimuli is known as the
     a. Freudian axiom
    *b. projective hypothesis
     c. Jungian axiom
     d. preconscious hypothesis

39. Which test below was originally developed to investigate the personality functioning of normal individuals?
     a. Rorschach test
     b. Personal Data Sheet
     c. Bernreuter Personality Inventory
    *d. Thematic Apperception Test

40. Which test below was originally developed to investigate the need for achievement? a. Rorschach test
     b. Personal Data Sheet
     c. Szondi test
    *d. Thematic Apperception Test

41. Which test below is clearly based upon wholly faulty premises?
     a. Rorschach test
    *b. Szondi test
     c. Bernreuter Personality Inventory
     d. Thematic Apperception Test

42. Which test is based upon the premise that projective preferences reveal recessive genes predisposing the individual for specific psychiatric disturbances?
    a. Rorschach test
    *b. Szondi test
    c. Bernreuter Personality Inventory
    d. Thematic Apperception Test

43. For which test below have clinicians mainly relied upon an impressionistic analysis for scoring?
    a. Rorschach test
    b. Personal Data Sheet
    c. Szondi test
    *d. Thematic Apperception Test

44. Which of the tests below has faded into oblivion?
    a. Rorschach test
    b. Personal Data Sheet
    *c. Szondi test
    d. Thematic Apperception Test

45. The famous Strong Vocational Interest Blank has roots that go back to the
    *a. Carnegie Interest Inventory
    b. Personal Data Sheet
    c. Thematic Apperception Test
    d. Minnesota Multiphasic Personality Inventory

46. Which test uses a forced-choice triad approach?
    a. Strong Vocational Interest Blank
    b. Personal Data Sheet
    *c. Kuder Preference Record
    d. Minnesota Multiphasic Personality Inventory

47. Founded in 1921, the first major test publishing firm was the
    a. Educational Testing Service
    *b. Psychological Corporation
    c. Science Research Associates
    d. Stanford Testing Corporation

Topic 2A

The Nature and Uses of Psychological Tests

Definition of a Test

Further Distinctions in Testing

Types of Tests

Uses of Testing

Case Exhibit 2.1: Test Results as Self-knowledge

Who May Obtain Tests

Sources of Information on Tests

Summary

Key Terms and Concepts

Classroom Discussion Questions

1. An interesting way to generate classroom discussion on the nature and definition of a test is to bring in one or more quasi-tests that can be found in any bookstore. For example, the Luscher Color Test or variations thereof can be found in most bookstores. After describing and demonstrating these tests, ask students to discuss whether they meet the criteria of a psychological test.

2. It is usually possible to create a lively debate by asking students who should have access to psychological tests. For example, should anyone be able to purchase a copy of the Wechsler Adult Intelligence Scale-Revised? Should a high school teacher who has taken a course on individual intelligence tests be allowed to administer the WAIS-R?

Extramural Assignments

1. A challenging assignment is to ask students to invent a test. Once they have selected a construct for measurement, they can be challenged to devise items and develop the test throughout the semester, paying special attention to the concepts introduced in the first few chapters of the text.

2. Students may gain insight into the ethics of testing if they are encouraged to poll others about the extent of cheating on standardized tests. It would be interesting to ask other students (anonymously, of course) to recount instances in which they or others cheated on any kind of standardized test, whether group or individual. Students could produce a brief catalog of these instances, discussing the likely effect on test validity, etc.

Classroom Demonstrations

1. The importance of standardized procedure is a topic worthy of demonstration. An easy way to approach this issue is to describe or demonstrate an existing test or subtest, and then ask students to

describe the probable effects of variations from standardized procedure. Digit span tests are especially useful in this regard. In addition to discussing the effects of nonstandard procedure, the instructor can demonstrate the effects. For example, students can be asked to write down orally presented digit sequences under various conditions: rapid reading (more than one digit per second), background noise (e.g., have a student cough several times during the presentation), meaningful sequences (e.g., 1-800-325-3535-1492-1776). By tallying class averages for these various conditions, the students can see the value of standardized procedures.

2. The textbook outlines eight different kinds of tests. For some of the tests in each category, it would be possible to demonstrate sample items. Instructors need to be sensitive to their own responsibilities, but it is usually possible to demonstrate tests without breaching test security. For example, college students can be shown sample items from the WISC-R with no harm; MMPI items can be read to show students the range of item types; the structure of interest inventories can be discussed without invaliding them; and so on.

3. This would be a good point to bring out the *Mental Measurements Yearbooks* and the *Test Critiques* volumes and circulate them in class. Also, The Journal of Psychoeducational Assessment and The Journal of Clinical Psychology are useful journals for demonstrating the kinds of research that new tests engender.

Essay Questions

1. Outline the characteristics of a test. Using a hypothetical test of your own invention, provide evidence that it is truly a test as defined in the textbook.

2. Discuss the potential uses of psychological tests.

3. Cite a new example of a behavioral assessment procedure.

TEST ITEM FILE

Topic 2A: The Nature and Uses of Psychological Tests

1. The _____ test is a multivariate assessment of heart rate, respiration, muscle tone, reflex irritability, and color in newborns.
   a. Reflex
   b. Newborn
   *c. Apgar
   d. Alpha

2. A specialist in psychology or education who develops and evaluates psychological tests:
   a. clinician
   *b. psychometrician
   c. psychometrist
   d. counselor

3. Which of the following could be a test, according to the definition offered in the textbook?
   a. a checklist for rating the social skills of a retarded youth
   b. a non-timed measure of mastery in adding pairs of three-digit numbers
   c. a microcomputer appraisal of reaction time
   *d. all of the above

4. Which of the following is NOT a typical characteristic of psychological tests?
   *a. standardization to a mean of 100
   b. sampling of behavior
   c. description of behavior with categories or scores
   d. use of norms to predict other behaviors

5. Tests that use a well-defined population of persons for their interpretive framework are referred to as:
   a. criterion-referenced
   b. population-referenced
   c. standard-referenced
   *d. norm-referenced

6. Criterion-referenced tests
   *a. measure what a person can do
   b. compare results to the performance levels of others
   c. are passed by everyone
   d. all of the above

7. Uniformity of administration procedures is the definition of
   a. criterion-referencing
   *b. standardization
   c. norm-referencing
   d. reliability

8. Which of the following is an essential step in the standardization of a test?
   a. use of identical stimuli with all examinees
   b. precise specification of oral instructions for subtests
   c. advice to the examiner as to how to handle queries from the examinee
   *d. all of the above

9. Why are tests merely a sample of behavior?
   *a. so that the time required for testing is not excessive
   b. a sample is as good as the totality of behaviors
   c. so that the examiner's influence is minimized
   d. because the examiner has a special interest in that sample of behavior

10. Suppose that answering "true" to the question "I drink a lot of water" happens to help predict depression. Would it be wise to include this item on a test used to identify depression?
    *a. yes, because the essential characteristic of a good test is that it predicts relevant behaviors
    b. no, because there is no theoretical link between drinking water and being depressed
    c. yes, because there is a theoretical link between drinking water and being depressed
    d. maybe, depending upon the theoretical orientation of the test developer

11. In the equation X = T + e, what is the best that a test developer can do?
   a. make T very large
   b. make T very small
   c. make e very large
   *d. make e very small

12. The norm group is referred to as the
   a. criterion sample
   *b. standardization sample
   c. reference group
   d. all of the above

13. The purpose of norms is to
   a. establish an average performance
   b. indicate the prevalence of high and low scores
   c. determine deviations from expectation
   *d. all of the above

14. The ability of a test to predict non-test behavior is determined by
   *a. an extensive body of postpublication validational research
   b. the scores of the standardization sample
   c. the reliability of the test
   d. the prepublication validational research

15. In a(n) _____ test, the objective is to determine where the examinee stands with respect to very tightly defined educational objectives.
   a. norm-referenced
   b. ability
   *c. criterion-referenced
   d. aptitude

16. Which is the most comprehensive term?
   a. testing
   b. scoring
   c. norming
   *d. assessing

17. The term _____ was invented during World War II to describe a program to select men for secret service assignment in the Office of Strategic Services.
    *a. assessment
    b. evaluation
    c. classification
    d. estimation

18. Which of the following was used as a situational test by the Office of Strategic Services during WWII?
    a. transporting equipment across a raging brook
    b. scaling a ten foot high wall
    c. surviving a realistic interrogation
    *d. all of the above

19. An important advantage of _____ tests is that the examiner can gauge the level of motivation of the examinee.
    a. group
    b. personality
    c. individual
    d. intelligence

20. Most intelligence tests use a _____ assortment of test items.
    a. homogeneous
    *b. heterogeneous
    c. random
    d. culture-free

21. _____ tests are often used to predict success in an occupation, training course, or educational endeavor.
    a. Intelligence
    b. Personality
    *c. Aptitude
    d. Achievement

22. _____ tests are often used to measure a person's degree of learning, success or accomplishment in a subject matter.
   a. Intelligence
   b. Personality
   c. Aptitude
   *d. Achievement

23. Measures of _____ emphasize novelty and originality in the solution of fuzzy problems or the production of artistic works.
   a. personality
   b. achievement
   *c. creativity
   d. femininity

24. Putting forth a variety of answers to a complex or fuzzy problem is an example of _____ thinking.
   *a. divergent
   b. convergent
   c. undisciplined
   d. intelligent

25. Checklists, inventories, and projective techniques are all examples of _____ tests.
   a. creativity
   b. intelligence
   *c. personality
   d. vocational

26. _____ share a common assumption that behavior is best understood in terms of clearly defined characteristics such as frequency, duration, antecedents, and consequences.
   a. Intelligence tests
   b. Personality inventories
   c. Creativity tests
   *d. Behavioral procedures

27. An A-B-C functional analysis refers to
    *a. Antecedents-Behaviors-Consequences
    b. Aptitudes-Behaviors-Creativity
    c. Achievement-Behavior-Consequence
    d. Analysis-Behavior-Consequence

28. The primary purpose of neuropsychological testing is to
    a. arrive at a neurological diagnosis
    *b. evaluate sensory, motor, cognitive, and behavioral strengths
and weaknesses
    c. determine the presence or absence of brain damage
    d. corroborate medical tests

29. A full neuropsychological assessment typically requires about how
long?
    a. an hour
    *b. three to eight hours
    c. two to three days
    d. four hours of testing on four separate days

30. By far the most common use of psychological tests is to
    *a. make decisions about persons
    b. diagnosis mental and emotional disorders
    c. determine personality functioning
    d. evaluate learning disabilities

31. Placement, screening, certification, and selection are all examples
of
    a. diagnosis
    b. program evaluation
    *c. classification
    d. research-based testing

32. When two tests can be used to select persons for two different
positions, the optimal strategy is
    *a. Use both tests in combination to finalize decisions
    b. Combine both tests into a single score
    c. Use the single tests with the highest predictive validity
    d. Take the best sections from each test to finalize decisions

33. In general, Head Start children show immediate gains in
  a. IQ
  b. school readiness
  c. academic achievement
  *d. all of the above

34. The purpose of the tilting-room-tilting-chair tests was to
  *a. analyze perceptual field dependence
  b. test airplane pilots during WWII
  c. assess motor reaction time
  d. all of the above

35. Access to psychological tests is restricted because:
  a. in the hands of unqualified persons, psychological tests can cause harm
  b. the selection process is rendered invalid for persons who preview test questions
  c. leakage of item content to the general public completely destroys the efficacy of a test
  *d. all of the above

36. Individual tests of intelligence, projective personality tests, and neuropsychological test batteries are examples of Level ___ tests.
  a. A
  b. B
  *c. C
  d. D

37. The best single reference source for information on mainstream tests is
  *a. the Mental Measurements Yearbook
  b. Psychological Abstracts
  c. Psychology Yearbook
  d. Journal of Consulting and Clinical Psychology

Topic 2B

The Testing Process

Standardized Procedures in Test Administration

Case Exhibit 2.2: A Worst Case Vignette of Non-Standard Testing

Desirable Procedures of Test Administration

Sensitivity to Disabilities

Desirable Procedures of Group Testing

Influence of the Examiner

   The Importance of Rapport
   Examiner Sex, Experience, and Race

Background and Motivation of the Examinee

   Test Anxiety
   Motivation to Deceive
   Effects of Coaching on Test Results

Issues in Scoring

Summary

Key Terms and Concepts

Classroom Discussion Questions

1. A useful way to begin Topic 2B is by asking students to catalogue the numerous ways in which test results can be swayed by extraneous factors. That is, other than the variable being measured, what other factors can cause test scores to be artificially high or low? It is especially helpful to have students provide specific examples.

2. Sensitivity to disabilities is another useful discussion topic. What kinds of disabilities might examinees possess? How might examiners recognize these disabilities? What adjustments are appropriate in response to a disability?

Extramural Assignments

1. Ask students to track down biographies, autobiographies, and journal articles about persons who were misdiagnosed by psychological tests because of unrecognized handicaps. The students could write a short synopsis or present a brief oral report to the class.

2. Divide the class into two to four groups and have each group collect data on a digit span task under different conditions. For example, the rate of presentation might be the independent variable, with different groups presenting at .5, 1.0, 1.5, and 2.0 seconds between digits. The groups could bring their data back to class and compare effects of varying the presentation methods.

Classroom Demonstrations

1. Subjective judgment in scoring can be demonstrated in class by reading students the criteria for a vocabulary item on the WISC-R or similar test and then asking students to rate various responses as 0, 1, or 2. Although there will usually be a high level of agreement, certain responses will prove difficult to score, with the result that ratings vary widely.

2. The importance of rapport can be demonstrated through role playing. The instructor can "test" several students with a hypothetical examination. By alternating demeanor between friendly and harsh, the effect of rapport can be demonstrated quite effectively.

3. Dozens of coaching manuals exist for the major achievement tests such as the SAT, GRE, and ACT. The cost is usually nominal, on the order of $5 - $10. These manuals provide an excellent starting point for classroom discussion on the nature of achievement testing, the construction of test items, the issue of guessing, the need for corrections for guessing, the problem of coaching, the quandary of teaching to the test, etc.

Essay Questions

1. Define test anxiety and summarize the research findings with respects to its correlates.

2. Describe desirable procedures for the administration of group tests.

3. Discuss the effects of coaching upon test results.

TEST ITEM FILE

Topic 2B: The Testing Process

1. Suppose a tester asks "What is a sofa?" and the child looks puzzled. In general, is it acceptable for the tester to rephrase the question, asking "What is a couch?"
    a. Yes, because valid testing requires the development of rapport
    b. Yes, because the two questions are equivalent
    c. No, because the tester should never deviate from standardized procedure
    *d. No, because the rephrased question is easier and therefore not comparable

2. In determining the boundaries of flexible testing procedures, the examiner should consider
   *a. how the test was likely administered to the norm sample
   b. the potential consequences of altering the test items
   c. the general dictum that testing procedures should be interpreted literally and strictly
   d. all of the above

3. In most cases, if a test question asks "What shape is a ball?" a correct answer would be recorded if
   a. the subject responds verbally "round"
   b. the subject responds verbally "spherical"
   c. the subject gestures with his index finger in a circular pattern
   *d. all of the above

4. The necessary prerequisite(s) to administering a new test:
   a. reading the manual
   b. memorizing key elements of instructions
   c. rehearsing the test
   *d. all of the above

5. The most likely cause of misdiagnosing mental retardation is:
   a. the IQ test is incorrectly scored
   *b. unknown to the tester, the subject is deaf or nearly deaf
   c. the examiner uses the wrong IQ test
   d. the subject was not feeling well during testing

6. Which age group is most prone to periodic accumulation of fluid in the middle ear during intervals of mild illness?
   *a. young subjects
   b. adolescents
   c. young adults
   d. old adults

7. Which of the following is a possible sign of hearing loss?
   a. inattentiveness
   b. poor articulation
   c. difficulty in following oral directions
   *d. all of the above

8. _____ persons often develop an "atypical attentive set" which causes them to concentrate on aspects of the test that the examiner may consider irrelevant.
    *a. hearing-impaired
    b. speech-impaired
    c. motor-impaired
    d. vision-impaired

9. Photophobia is a condition in which the individual is
    a. afraid of visually-loaded tests
    *b. unusually sensitive to bright lights
    c. afraid of psychological tests in general
    d. none of the above

10. Owing to the special nature of this kind of impairment, subjects may receive less credit on a test item than is due.
    a. hearing-impaired
    *b. speech-impaired
    c. motor-impaired
    d. vision-impaired

11. When testing a person with a mild motor handicap, examiners may wish to omit
    a. multiple choice spatial items
    b. untimed spatial items
    *c. timed performance subtests
    d. all of the above

12. According to experts on group testing (e.g., Traxler, 1951), which kind of test generally requires the greatest vigilance from the examiner?
    *a. group test
    b. individual test
    c. group and individual tests require equal vigilance
    d. unknown

13. Undoubtedly the single greatest source of error in group test administration is:
   a. reading the wrong instructions
   b. giving the wrong form of the test
   c. giving a test to the wrong age group
   *d. incorrect timing of tests

14. Which of the following is important for valid administration of group tests?
   a. a pleasant and well illuminated testing room
   b. absence of disruptive noise
   c. an appropriate writing surface
   *d. all of the above

15. In general, how do test manuals for group standardized tests handle the issue of guessing?
   *a. they provide explicit instructions to examinees as to the advantages and potential pitfalls of guessing
   b. they warn examinees that guessing is usually counterproductive
   c. most commonly, the test manual does not provide any guidance on the pros and cons of guessing
   d. they explain that guessing seldom improves the examinee's score

16. Suppose a young girl answers correctly on 37 questions from a 50-item test but answers erroneously on 9 questions, leaving 2 questions blank. Suppose their are four alternatives per question. Using established principles of probability, what would be her corrected score?
   a. 32   c. 36
   *b. 34   d. 37

17. The test item writer's aim is to make all or nearly all considered guesses _____ guesses
   a. correct
   *b. wrong
   c. random
   d. educated

18. When testing children, testing should begin
    a. not longer than 5 to 10 minutes after the child arrives
    b. when the test manual says it should begin
    *c. when he/she seems relaxed enough to give maximum effort
    d. almost immediately so as to prevent the child from
developing fear of the tester

19. Which of the examiner characteristics listed below has been
found to make a consistent and significant difference in the outcome
of individual test results?
    a. sex
    b. experience
    c. race
    *d. none of the above

20. In one study reported in the text (Terrell et al. 1981), mistrustful
blacks performed relatively poorly when tested by _____ examiners.
    a. black
    *b. white
    c. black or white
    d. female

21. What is the relationship between test anxiety and school
achievement?
    *a. high anxiety correlates with low achievement
    b. high anxiety correlates with high achievement
    c. test anxiety and school achievement are unrelated
    d. the relationship between test anxiety and school
achievement is unknown

22. Test-anxious students have study habits that are
_____ those of other students.
    a. far superior to
    b. slightly superior to
    c. about equally effective as
    *d. worse than

23. When instructions for a task are neutral or nonthreatening, test-anxious subjects
    *a. perform just as well as low-anxious subjects
    b. show a decrement in performance
    c. still perceive the situation to be stressful
    d. all of the above

24. Suppose subjects are matched on overall IQ. On timed subtests from an intelligence scale such as the WAIS, the performance of low-anxious subjects _____ that of high-anxious subjects.
    a. drops below
    b. equals
    *c. surpasses
    d. is twice as fast as

25. Conscious faking on psychological tests is thought to be
    *a. rare
    b. common place
    c. evidence of psychopathology
    d. blatant and obvious

26. On tests such as the GRE, what is the effect of several hours of self-tutoring on test scores?
    a. no documented gain
    b. a mere 10 point increase
    *c. a gain of about 50 points
    d. a gain of 100 or more points

27. The effects of coaching on aptitude tests are
    *a. highly specific
    b. nonexistent
    c. generalizable
    d. unpredictable

28. What has been the response of most test developers to the challenge posed by coaching?
　　*a. they now provide sample test materials to prospective examinees
　　b. they have redoubled their efforts to produce parallel forms of existing tests
　　c. they have ignored the problem altogether
　　d. they have encouraged subjects to buy coaching manuals

29. Examiner judgments about scoring--whether a certain response on an IQ test merits 1 or 2 raw score points, for example--are
　　a. never required on the best tests
　　b. a major source of scoring errors
　　*c. rarely a significant source of scoring errors
　　d. typically decided by a coin toss

30. On an individually administered IQ test, how often would two psychologists derive exactly the same score from the same test protocol?
　　a. always
　　b. most of the time
　　*c. rarely
　　d. never

Topic 3A

Norms and Test Standardization

Case Exhibit 3.1 Outmoded Tests and Outdated Norms

Raw Scores

Essential Statistical Concepts

Frequency Distributions
Measures of Central Tendency
Measures of Variability
The Normal Distribution
Skewness

Raw Score Transformations

Percentiles and Percentile Ranks
Standard Scores
T Scores And Other Standardized Scores
Normalizing Standard Scores
Stanines, Stens, and C Scale
A Summary of Statistically Based Norms

Selecting a Norm Group

Age and Grade Norms
Local and Subgroup Norms
Expectancy Tables

Criterion-Referenced Tests

Summary

Key Terms and Concepts

Classroom Discussion Questions

1. The distinctions between mean, median, and mode are worthy of classroom discussion. The instructor could portray different distributions of scores on the blackboard and ask students to compute mean, median and mode. More important, students need to understand why the median is often the preferred index of central tendency--so be sure and provide one distribution of scores that is highly skewed. For example:

10, 10, 10, 10, 12, 20, 21, 22, 28, 35, 36, 37, 47, 48, 54

The mean of this distribution is 26.66; the median ia a more representative 22; yet, the most typical score is the mode of 10. Which is the best index?

2. We operate in a norm-oriented society--so much so that students take this state of affairs for granted. A useful discussion question is why criterion-referenced tests aren't used more often. Have students discuss what a criterion-referenced test would look like for this course. Should criterion-referenced tests become the "norm"?

Extramural Assignments

1. One of the issues raised by Topic 3A is whether the normal distribution is an inherent characteristic of nature or a human-made artifact. Although the project would require some effort, students might be encouraged to pick one or more measurable human characteristics and collect a very large sample of data to determine whether the distribution of scores is normal or near-normal in appearance. In order to obtain an appropriately large sample of data, teams of researchers might be asked to share in data collection. Two characteristics that should be of interest to psychology students: motor speed (a simple index is to ask subject to put their hand flat on the table top and tap with the index finger as many times as possible in a timed thirty second trial); and, head circumference (simply measure with a cloth tape).

2. To become familiar with the many ways in which normative data are presented, students could be asked to obtain samples of normative data from research studies and test manuals. The Journal of Psychoeducational Assessment and The Journal of Clinical Psychology both publish preliminary versions of new assessment instruments, complete with tentative standardization data.

Classroom Demonstrations

1. Students often have only the vaguest understanding of the distinction between reliability and validity. A good way to clarify the distinction is to describe the Gregory Intelligence Test (GIT) and ask whether it is reliable and also ask whether it is valid. The GIT is scored as follows: count the number of letters in a person's last name, and multiply by 10 to obtain the IQ. For example, Gregory scores an IQ of 70 on the GIT, which is borderline retarded; Csikszentmihalyi scores an IQ of 160 on the GIT, which is easily in the genius range. Is the GIT reliable? (Yes, the test-retest correlation for GIT scores would be 1.00). Is the GIT valid? (No, it does not measure what it purports to measure).

2. The computation of a reliability coefficient can be demonstrated in class quite easily. Using the same finger tapping test described above, each student could provide test and retest scores for the instructor to portray on the blackboard. Computation of the Pearson *r* test-retest coefficient could be done on the spot. Factors which influence reliability can also be demonstrated. For example, test and retest could be done with 30 second trials and also with 10 second trails. Reliability for the former should be higher, demonstrating that a test with more "items" is generally more reliable than a test with fewer items.

3. Darrell Huff's *How to Lie With Statistics* contains many excellent demonstrations of how statistics can be purposefully or inadvertently misleading.

Essay Questions

1. Discuss the relative merits of the following indices of central tendency: mean, median, mode.

2. What is the difference between percent correct and percentile rank?

3. Draw a normal curve and show percentages between the curve at plus and minus 1, 2, and 3 standard deviations from the mean.

4. What is an expectancy table? Portray a realistic example of an expectancy table.

TEST ITEM FILE

Topic 3A: Norms and Test Standardization

1. The initial outcome of testing is typically a
     *a. raw score
     b. scaled score
     c. subscale score
     d. transformed score

2. A sample of examinees who are representative of the population for whom the test is intended is called a _____ group.
     a. reference
     b. criterion
     *c. norm
     d. stratified

3. Percentile ranks, age equivalents, grade equivalents, and standard scores are all examples of
     *a. norms
     b. non-linear transformations
     c. normal distributions
     d. all of the above

4. For criterion-referenced tests, norms are
   a. essential
   b. common but not essential
   *c. uncommon and not essential
   d. common and essential

5. In a frequency distribution, the sums of the frequencies for all intervals will _____ the total number of scores in the sample.
   a. exceed
   *b. equal
   c. be less than
   d. be less than or equal to

6. In a _____ the frequency of the class intervals is represented by single points rather than columns.
   a. histogram
   b. frequency table
   *c. frequency polygon
   d. scattergram

7. It is common for frequency distributions to include between _____ class intervals.
   a. three and five
   b. three and eight
   c. five and ten
   *d. five and fifteen

8. In a smooth but skewed distribution, the most representative measure of central tendency is the
   a. mean
   *b. median
   c. mode
   d. quartile

9. The middlemost score when all the scores have been ranked is called the
   a. mean
   *b. median
   c. mode
   d. second quartile

10. If the number of scores is even, the median is
   *a. the average of the middlemost two scores
   b. the higher of the middlemost two scores
   c. the lower of the middlemost two scores
   d. cannot be computed

11. The most frequently occurring score is the
   a. mean
   b. median
   *c. mode
   d. all of the above

12. Consider the case where nine persons earn $10,000 and a tenth person earns $990,000. What is their average income?
   a. $99,000
   b. $111,000
   c. $10,000
   *d. $100,000

13. The most commonly used statistical index of variability in a group of scores is the
   a. range
   b. variance
   *c. standard deviation
   d. none of the above

14. The Greek symbol "sigma" stands for
   a. mean
   *b. sum of
   c. correlation
   d. difference

15. A small x is used to designate
   a. the mean
   b. correlation
   c. individual scores
   *d. deviation scores

16. What is the relationship between the variance and the standard deviation?
   a. they are completely unrelated
   b. they are usually correlated to a modest degree
   *c. one can be computed from the other
   d. one is the inverse of the other

17. For which kind of distribution would the highest number of persons score in the superior range?
   a. rectangular
   *b. normal
   c. platonic
   d. kurtic

18. Why do psychologists prefer the normal distribution?
   a. it has useful features for statistical inference
   b. it can be defined with mathematical precision
   c. it often arises spontaneously in nature
   *d. all of the above

19. In a normal distribution, approximately _____ percent of the scores will exceed the mean by two standard deviations.
   *a. 2
   b. 5
   c. 10
   d. 25

20. In a normal distribution, approximately _____ percent of the scores will fall within one standard deviation of the mean in either direction.
   a. 28   *c. 68
   b. 48   d. 88

21. In his initial investigations, Wechsler consider the belief that mental measures must distribute themselves according to the normal curve to be
   a. axiomatic
   b. probably correct
   c. mistaken
   d. merely an hypothesis

22. If test scores are piled up at the low end of the scale, the distribution is said to be
    a. negatively skewed
    *b. positively skewed
    c. leptokurtic
    d. platykurtic

23. The distribution of mental test scores in standardization samples typically
    *a. approximates a normal curve
    b. is negatively skewed
    c. is positively skewed
    d. is bimodal

24. In psychological testing, skewed distributions usually signify that the test developer has
    a. a bias that favors one or more subgroups of persons
    b. purposely set out to produce a test with skewness
    c. underestimated the ability of some subjects
    *d. included too few easy items or too few hard items

25. When initial research indicates that an instrument produces skewed results in the standardization sample, test developers typically
    a. use a statistical transformation
    *b. revamp the test at the item level
    c. obtain data from a second sample
    d. all of the above

26. Suppose a subject scored at the 94th percentile on a psychological test? What does that mean?
    a. the subject answered 94 percent of the questions correctly
    *b. the subject's score exceeded 94 percent of the standardization sample
    c. the subject's score exceeded 6 percent of the standardization sample
    d. none of the above

27. A percentile of 25 is often denoted as
    a. Q25
    b. Q75
    *c. Q1
    d. none of the above

28. Percentile scores have one major drawback:
    a. they are difficult for most persons to comprehend
    b. they often sum to more than 100 percent
    c. an examinee's percentile score fluctuates significantly
    *d. they distort the underlying measurement scale

29. The difference in underlying raw score points between percentiles of 90 and 99 is _____ that between percentiles of 50 and 59.
    *a. greater than
    b. less than
    c. the same as
    d. of unknown relation to

30. A _____ uses the standard deviation of the total distribution of raw scores as the fundamental unit of measurement.
    a. percentile
    b. percentile rank
    *c. standard score
    d. T-score

31. A z-score is the same thing as a
    a. percentile
    b. percentile rank
    *c. standard score
    d. T-score

32. Suppose a group of scores has a mean of 40 and a standard deviation of 10. A score of 80 would equate to a standard score of
    a. 1.0
    b. 2.0
    *c. 4.0
    d. 8.0

33. A group of standard scores always possesses a mean of ___ and a standard deviation of ___.
    a. 1.0, 1.0
    b. 1.0, 10.0
    *c. 0.0, 1.0
    d. 0.0, 10.0

34. Suppose that a college freshman earned 125 raw score points on a vocabulary test where the normative sample averaged 100 points (with SD of 15 points). Suppose, in addition, he earned 110 raw score points on a spatial thinking test where the normative sample averaged 90 points (with SD of 20 points). In which skill area does he show greater aptitude, vocabulary or spatial thinking?
    *a. vocabulary
    b. spatial thinking
    c. aptitude is equal in the two areas
    d. insufficient data to answer the question

35. For which type(s) of scores are negative values possible?
    *a. standard score
    b. standardized scores
    c. neither a nor b
    d. both a and b

36. The mean of a standardized score is typically set at
    a. 100
    b. 500
    c. 50
    *d. all of the above

37. T score scales are especially common for _____ tests.
    a. intelligence
    *b. personality
    c. achievement
    d. aptitude

38. To eliminate negative scores, the pre-selected mean of a standardized score should be at least _____ times as large as the standard deviation.
   a. two   *c. five
   b. three   d. ten

39. The most popular approach for normalizing standard scores is conversion of
   *a. percentiles to normalized standard scores
   b. raw scores to T scores
   c. T scores to raw scores
   d. percentiles to percentile ranks

40. The use of normalized standard scores is appropriate when
   a. the normative sample is large and representative
   b. the raw score distribution is only mildly non-normal
   *c. both a and b
   d. neither a nor b

41. In a _____ scale, all raw scores are converted to a single-digit system of scores ranging from 1 to 9.
   *a. stanine
   b. sten
   c. C
   d. digit

42. The mean of _____ scores is always 5, and the standard deviation is approximately 2.
   *a. stanine
   b. sten
   c. C
   d. digit

43. The restriction imposed by Hollerith cards was a main impetus for the development of _____ scales.
   *a. stanine
   b. sten
   c. C
   d. digit

44. A C scale consists of _____ units.
   a. 9
   b. 10
   *c. 11
   d. 100

45. A WAIS-R IQ of 115 could also be reported as a
   a. standard score of +1.00
   b. T score of 60
   c. percentile rank of 84
   *d. all of the above

46. What approach do test developers use in selecting a standardization sample?
   a. they use a strictly random sample
   b. they use a pure strategy of stratified random sampling
   *c. they make a good faith effort to find a representative sample
   d. they pick samples on an opportunistic basis

47. Which kind of norms are appropriate for aptitude tests?
   *a. age norms
   b. grade norms
   c. both age and grade norms
   d. neither age nor grade norms

48. For what purpose might ethnic norms for standardized intelligence tests be superior to nationally based norms?
   *a. for predicting competence within the child's non-school environment
   b. for predicting performance within mainstream schools
   c. for predicting college performance in mostly white schools
   d. all of the above

49. A tabular depiction of the established relationship between test scores and expected outcome on a relevant task is known as a(n)
   a. correlation coefficient
   b. histogram
   c. frequency polygon
   *d. expectancy table

Topic 3B

Concepts of Reliability

Case Exhibit 3.2: Test Reliability and Courtroom Testimony

Classical Theory and the Sources of Measurement Error

Sources of Measurement Error

Item Selection
Test Administration
Test Scoring
Systematic Measurement Error

Measurement Error and Reliability

The Reliability Coefficient

The Correlation Coefficient

Computation of the Correlation Coefficient

The Correlation Coefficient as a Reliability Coefficient

Reliability as Temporal Stability

Test-Retest Reliability
Alternate-Forms Reliability

Reliability as Internal Consistency

Split-Half Reliability
The Spearman-Brown Formula
Critique of the Split-Half Approach
Coefficient Alpha
The Kuder-Richardson Estimate of Reliability
Inter-Scorer Reliability

Classroom Discussion Questions

1. The idea that a psychological measurement always incorporates measurement error is a new one to most students. A useful discussion approach is to bring a specific test or subtest to class and ask students to brainstorm on the potential sources of measurement error for that test. For example, the instructor might bring a WISC-R subtest to class, demonstrate its administration and scoring, and ask for discussion of sources of measurement error. Once a list is compiled, these could be compared to the categories mentioned in the textbook.

2. Students usually have anecdotal horror stories about nonstandard testing conditions. Ask them to report instances in which the conditions of testing may have affected the accuracy of test scores.

3. This topic introduces numerous different methods for estimating the reliability of measurement. The instructor can generate much discussion by asking students first to summarize these methods, then to discuss which method(s) would be appropriate for the following kinds of "tests":

  finger tapping speed
  timed typing test
  galvanic skin response to a loud noise
  essay examination
  multiple choice examination
  timed test of "cancelling e's" from text
  personality scale measuring depression

Extramural Assignments

1. Ask students to pick a favorite or interesting test and then consult the *Mental Measurements Yearbook* to determine how reliability was assessed for that test as well as to report the typical range for reliability coefficients.

2. Ask students to pick a favorite or interesting test and then consult the *Mental Measurements Yearbook* to determine the standard error

of measurement for that test. Have students discuss the implications of standard error of measurement for decision making with that test.

Classroom Demonstrations

1. Divide the class randomly into two halves. Develop ideal and difficult conditions of administration for the same test. The test could be one that you devise--e.g., a series of complex multiplications--or an existing test--e.g., digit span administered orally with responses given by paper and pencil. Then, one half of the class takes the test under quiet, well-lighted conditions, whereas the other half of the class takes the test under conditions of adversity. (For example, play loud music, turn the lights on and off). Scores under the adverse conditions should be lower, illustrating one component of measurement error and its effect upon reliability.

2. To illustrate a "test" that has zero reliability, do some form of ESP study in class in a test-retest format. Draw a scatterplot on the blackboard to depict the absence of relationship between first and second test scores.

Essay Questions

1. Outline the assumptions of the classical theory of measurement.

2. Describe the major methods for estimating the reliability of a test. Discuss the conditions under which each method is appropriate or inappropriate.

3. Discuss reliability in relation to criterion-referenced tests.

4. Define and discuss standard error of measurement.

TEST ITEM FILE

Topic 3B: Concepts of Reliability

1. The classical theory of reliability is also known as the theory of
    a. consistency
    b. general and specific factors
    *c. true and error scores
    d. generalizability

2. Errors of measurement are
    a. positive
    b. negative
    *c. positive or negative
    d. none of the above

3. Regarding the true score, which statement is correct?
    a. we can never know the true score with certainty
    b. we can derive a probability that the true scores resides within a certain interval
    c. we can derive a best estimate of the true score
    *d. all of the above

4. Typically, errors of measurement arise from
    a. item selection
    b. test administration
    c. test scoring
    *d. all of the above

5. The particular choice of items on a test is _____ a source of measurement error in psychological testing.
    *a. always
    b. usually
    c. rarely
    d. never

6. _____ measurement errors arise when a test consistently measures something other than the trait for which it was intended.
- a. Random
- *b. Systematic
- c. Unsystematic
- d. Probabilistic

7. Unsystematic measurement errors behave like _____ variables.
- a. predictable
- *b. random
- c. discrete
- d. functional

8. Reliability and measurement error are
- a. unrelated
- b. moderately correlated
- *c. related in a precise statistical manner
- d. none of the above

9. The sources of measurement error are
- a. mysterious and unknown
- *b. potentially knowable for individual cases
- c. of no significance in test development
- d. all of the above

10. Measurement errors
- a. are equally likely to be positive or negative
- b. will average out to zero across a large group of subjects
- c. act as random influences
- *d. all of the above

11. Classical theory assumes that measurement errors
- *a. are not correlated with true scores
- b. usually penalize the subject
- c. are correlated from one test to the next
- d. can be determined for the individual subject

12. The variance of obtained scores is
   a. the variance of true scores minus the variance of errors of measurement
   *b. the variance of true scores plus the variance of errors of measurement
   c. The variance of errors of measurement minus the variance of true scores
   d. none of the above

13. The value of a reliability coefficient can vary between
   a. -1.0 and +1.0
   *b. 0.0 and +1.0
   c. 0.0 and 0.9
   d. two numbers that depend upon the underlying units of measurement

14. Correlations of +1.0 are extremely rare in psychological research and usually signify
   a. an important breakthrough
   b. computational error
   *c. a trivial finding
   d. a false relationship

15. If scores on ability tests A and B are negatively correlated, this usually means that
   *a. scores on one of the tests are reported as errors
   b. abilities measured by the two tests are unrelated
   c. high ability on one test is associated with low ability on the other
   d. all of the above

16. In a sample of adults, correlations between reaction time and weight would most likely be
   a. strongly positive
   b. strongly negative
   c. close to zero
   d. close to +1.0

17. The Pearson r correlation coefficient takes into account
    a. each subject's ranking on the first and second variable
    b. the amount of each subject's deviation above or below the
group mean
    *c. both a and b
    d. neither a nor b

18. The formula for the correlation coefficient utilizes
    a. the sums of the squared deviations
    b. the number of subjects
    c. the standard deviations of the X and Y scores
    *d. all of the above

19. Methods for computing the reliability coefficient for a test involve
    a. temporal stability
    b. internal consistency
    *c. both a and b
    d. neither a nor b

20. If all other factors are held constant, what effect does a strong
practice effect have upon a test's reliability?
    *a. none
    b. decreases the reliability
    c. increases the reliability
    d. reduces reliability to near zero

21. Which of the below is an index of the internal consistency of a test
or scale?
    a. test-retest
    b. alternate forms
    *c. split-half
    d. none of the above

22. The most common method for obtaining split halves of a test is to
compare scores on
    a. the first and second half of the test
    *b. the odd and even items of the test
    c. randomly divided halves of the test
    d. none of the above

23. The Pearson r between two halves of a test will usually _____ the reliability of the full instrument.
    a. overestimate
    b. approximate
    *c. underestimate
    d. none of the above

24. For which kind of reliability is the Spearman-Brown formula relevant?
    a. test-retest
    b. alternate forms
    *c. split-half
    d. none of the above

25. A half-test reliability of .7 is equivalent to an estimated full test reliability of about
    a. .7   c. .9
    *b. .8   d, 1.0

26. The mean of the split-half coefficients resulting from all possible splittings of a test is known as
    a. Pearson r
    *b. coefficient alpha
    c. mean reliability
    d. none of the above

27. Which coefficient is used to gauge the degree to which a test measures a single factor?
    a. Pearson r
    *b. coefficient alpha
    c. mean reliability
    d. none of the above

28. When is the Kuder-Richardson formula useful?
    a. for split-half estimates
    b. when coefficient alpha cannot be used
    c. for alternate forms of a test
    *d. when test items are scored 0 or 1

29. Which form of reliability does not assess the potential temporal stability of test scores?
    *a. inter-scorer
    b. test-retest
    c. alternate forms
    d. parallel forms

30. Generalizability theory is an example of
    a. a direct approach to validity
    *b. a domain sampling approach to reliability
    c. a test-retest approach to reliability
    d. an alternate forms approach to reliability

31. In generalizability theory, test forms, observers and, occasions are all examples of
    a. domains
    b. variables
    c. samples
    *d. facets

32. A _____ test typically contains items of uniform and generally simple level of difficulty.
    *a. speed
    b. power
    c. screening
    d. ceiling

33. A _____ test allows enough time for test takers to attempt all items, but is constructed so that no test taker is able to obtain a perfect score.
    a. speed
    *b. power
    c. screening
    d. ceiling

34. The reliability of a speed test should be based on the
    a. odd-even method
    b. screening method
    c. reaction time method
    *d. test-retest method

35. Correlations based upon a homogeneous subset of subjects tend to be lower than for the entire group. This is known as
   a. correlation shrinkage
   b. power testing
   *c. restriction of range
   d. none of the above

36. With _____, traditional approaches to the assessment of reliability are simply inappropriate.
   *a. criterion-referenced tests
   b. power tests
   c. screening tests
   d. all of the above

37. Many authors suggest that reliability should be at least ___ for decisions about individuals.
   a. .60   c. .80
   b. .70   *d. .90

38. The standard deviation of an examinee's hypothetical obtained scores on a large number of equivalent tests is known as the
   a. standard error of the difference
   b. deviation score
   c. standard error of the mean
   *d. standard error of measurement

39. What is required to compute the standard error of measurement?
   *a. reliability coefficient and SD of the test scores
   b. SD of the test scores and validity coefficient
   c. reliability coefficient and N of subjects
   d. SD of the test scores and N of subjects

40. Full Scale IQ is ____ percent certain to be accurate within plus or minus 5 IQ points.
   a. 80
   b. 90
   *c. 95
   d. 100

41. If an examinee obtains a verbal score higher than his/her
performance score, then the underlying true scores for verbal and
performance abilities
    a. must always show the same pattern
    b. almost always show the same pattern
  *c. may or may not show the same pattern
    d. are equivalent to the obtained scores

42. The standard error of the difference is used to determine
    a. if an obtained score is close to the true score
  *b. whether the difference between two scores is significant
    c. the likely degree of measurement error for a score
    d. none of the above

Topic 4A

Basic Concepts of Validity

Case Exhibit 4.1: Research as the Essential Proof of Test Validity

Validity: A Definition

Content Validity

Quantification of Content Validity
Face Validity

Criterion-Related Validity

Characteristics of a Good Criterion
Concurrent Validity
Predictive Validity
Validity Coefficient and the Standard Error of the Estimate
Decision Theory Applied to Psychological Tests
Taylor-Russell Tables

Construct Validity

Approaches to Construct Validity

Test Homogeneity
Appropriate Developmental Changes
Theory-Consistent Group Differences
Theory-Consistent Intervention Effects
Convergent and Discriminant Validation
Factor Analysis

Extra-Validity Concerns and the Widening Scope of Test Validity

Unintended Side Effects of Testing
The Lake Wobegon Effect: Social Consequences of
Standardized Testing

The Widening Scope of Test Validity

Summary

Key Terms and Concepts

Classroom Discussion Questions

1. Propose to the students that you have developed a hypothetical test of resilience, the capacity to continue functioning in spite of adversity. (You may want to define the construct in even greater detail.) Discuss with the students what kind of evidence would be needed to establish the construct validity of your new test.

2. Scholastic aptitude tests should possess good predictive validity. Have the students discuss the kinds of proof that could be offered as to the predictive validity of a scholastic aptitude test. It might be useful to introduce the notion of false positives (students falsely predicted to succeed) and false negatives (students falsely predicted to fail) as well, to illustrate the role of values in the ultimate assessment of a test's validity.

Extramural Assignments

1. One important concept introduced in this topic is the notion of a regression equation for purposes of prediction. Ask students to dig through research literature to find various regression equations. These could be introduced in class and the various components discussed.

2. Another important concept introduced in this topic is the notion of false positive/false negative. Have students write up the consequences of false positives and false negatives for the following test-based decisions:

    whether a law enforcement candidate is prone to using excessive
        force
    whether a client is suicidal
    whether a third grader is learning disabled
    whether an employed aircraft mechanic is a safety risk to the
        company

In each case, which is worse, a false positive or a false negative? Which should we try to minimize?

3. Regarding the "Lake Wobegon Effect," ask students to survey teachers regarding the use of nationally normed achievement tests. The students could construct a brief questionnaire asking, e.g., whether there is any pressure to "teach to the test" and so forth.

Classroom Demonstrations

1. Bring to class the latest edition of the Standards for Educational and Psychological Measurement. Cite several of the specific standards and discuss how they apply to individual tests.

2. Bring a test to class and discuss th+e validity evidence for that test as presented in the manual. A good test for this purpose is the Kaufman Assessment Battery for Children.

Essay Questions

1. Define and discuss the application of a Taylor-Russell table.

2. Summarize the kinds of evidence that might be presented to substantiate the construct validity of a test.

3. Write a realistic regression equation that summarizes the prediction of first-semester college grade point average from an Academic Aptitude Test (AAT) and Personal Motivation Test (PMT). Describe and discuss the components of the equation.

4. Define content validity. Give an example of how the content validity of a spelling test might be guaranteed.

5. What does it mean to say that a criterion measure should be from from contamination?

6. What is the "Lake Wobegon Effect" and how does it arise?

7. Define the functionalist perspective on test validity. How does it differ from the traditional perspective?

TEST ITEM FILE

Topic 4A: Basic Concepts of Validity

1. What is the relationship between the reliability and the validity of a psychological test?
   a. none; these concepts are separate and independent
   *b. reliability is necessary but not sufficient for validity
   c. reliability is necessary and sufficient for validity
   d. validity is a necessary precursor to reliability

2. A test is valid when the inferences made from it are
   a. appropriate
   b. meaningful
   c. useful
   *d. all of the above

3. Traditionally, the different ways of accumulating validity evidence have been grouped into three categories:
   *a. content, criterion-related, and construct validity
   b. face, criterion-related, and construct validity
   c. face, content, and construct validity
   d. content, concurrent, and predictive validity

4. The degree to which items on a test are representative of the universe of behavior the test was designed to sample is an index of _____ validity
   *a. content
   b. concurrent
   c. predictive
   d. construct

5. When are expert judges are needed to determine the content validity of a test?
   a. always
   *b. when the trait being measured is ill-defined
   c. when the trait being measured is highly technical
   d. all of the above

6. Content validity can be quantified if
    a. the test developer has access to thousands of subjects
    *b. two or more judges assess the relevance of all test items
    c. the test developer performs a factor analysis on the
response matrix
    d. all of the above

7. A test has _____ validity if it looks valid to test users,
examiners, and especially the examinees.
    a. content
    *b. face
    c. criterion-related
    d. construct

8. The only reason for building in _____ validity involves public
relations.
    a. content
    *b. face
    c. criterion-related
    d. construct

9. A _____ is any outcome measure against which a test is
validated.
    a. response
    b. behavior
    *c. criterion
    d. index variable10.In test validation, criteria should be
    a. reliable
    b. appropriate
    c. free from contamination
    *d. all of the above

10. The theoretical upper limit of the validity coefficient is constrained
by the reliability of
    a. the test
    b. the criterion
    *c. both the test and the criterion
    d. neither the test nor the criterion

11. In test validation studies, criterion measures should incorporate items that are _____ to the test items.
   a. highly similar
   b. identical
   c. completely unrelated
   *d. none of the above

12. Correlations between a new test and existing tests are often cited as evidence of _____ validity.
   a. content
   *b. concurrent
   c. predictive
   d. construct

13. In _____ validity, test scores are used to estimate outcome measures obtained at a later date.
   a. content   *c. predictive
   b. concurrent   d. construct

14. _____ validity is particularly relevant for entrance examinations and employment tests.
   a. Content
   b. Concurrent
   *c. Predictive
   d. Construct

15. When tests are used for purposes of _____, it is necessary to develop a regression equation.
   *a. predicting outcomes
   b. validating a theory
   c. content validation
   d. estimating reliability

16. Most likely, the regression equation $Y = .07X + .2$ describes
   a. a smooth curve
   *b. a best-fitting straight line
   c. estimated IQ
   d. the band of error

17. The standard error of the estimate is an index of the error of measurement caused by the _____ of a test.
    a. unreliability
    *b. imperfect validity
    c. sampling restriction
    d. standardization sample

18. Suppose the standard error of the estimate for predicted grade point average (GPA) is 0.2 grade units. Suppose a student has a predicted GPA of 2.90. Approximately what is the probability that the student will achieve a GPA of 3.3 or higher?
    a. .5 percent
    *b. 2.5 percent
    c. 10 percent
    d. cannot be computed

19. In decision theory, persons who are predicted to succeed but who fail are known as
    a. false positives
    *b. false negatives
    c. true positives
    d. true negatives

20. Formula for the hit rate is
    a. (misses)/(hits + misses)
    *b. (hits)/(hits + misses)
    c. (hits + misses)/(misses)
    d. (hits + misses)/(hits)

21. Proponents of decision theory make the following fundamental assumption(s):
    a. the value of various outcomes to the institution can be expressed in terms of a common scale
    b. the most generally useful strategy is one which maximizes the average gain or minimizes average loss
    *c. both a and b
    d. neither a nor b

22. In order to use the Taylor-Russell tables, the tester must specify:
   a. the predictive validity of the test
   b. the selection ratio
   c. the base rate for successful applicants
   *d. all of the above

23. Suppose we have a test with low predictive validity. Under what condition can the Taylor-Russell tables be used to improve selection accuracy with this test?
   a. none--nothing can rescue a test with low predictive validity
   b. when there is a large sample of subjects
   c. when the time interval between selection and outcome is very brief
   *d. when the selection ratio is very low

24. A construct is
   *a. a theoretical, intangible quality or trait in which individuals differ
   b. any variable which permits precise measurement
   c. essentially synonymous with a concept
   d. all of the above

25. A construct possesses the following characteristic(s):
   a. it cannot be operationally defined
   b. a network of predictions can be derived from theory about the construct
   *c. both a and b
   d. neither a nor b

26. Many psychometric theorists regard _____ validity as the unifying concept for all types of validity evidence.
   a. content   c. predictive
   b. concurrent   *d. construct

27. Internal consistency is roughly synonymous with
   a. trait stability
   *b. homogeneity
   c. item-total independence
   d. all of the above

28. The construct validity of a vocabulary test would be buttressed if scores _____ with increasing age.
    *a. increased
    b. decreased
    c. remained stable
    d. increased and then decreased

29. "Interest in and concern for others" defines
    a. altruism
    b. sociability
    c. extraversion
    *d. social interest

30. Suppose a new measure of extraversion possesses a negligible correlation with intelligence. This would be support for _____ validity.
    a. convergent
    *b. discriminant
    c. content
    d. concurrent

31. In the multi-trait multi-method matrix, the correlations down the main diagonal are _____ coefficients.
    *a. reliability   c. error
    b. validity   d. regression

32. A multi-trait multi-method matrix provides information about
    a. reliability
    b. convergent validity
    c. discriminant validity
    *d. all of the above

33. The goal in factor analysis is to find a smaller set of dimensions, called _____, that can account for the observed array of intercorrelations among individual tests.
    a. loadings
    *b. factors
    c. rotations
    d. iterations

34. How many separate correlations can be computed between 10 tests?
    a. 10
   *b. 45
    c. 90
    d. 100

35. A factor loading is actually a(n)
    a. beta weight
   *b. correlation
    c. eigenvalue
    d. all of the above

36. Factor loadings can vary between
    a. 0 and 100
   *b. -1.0 and +1.0
    c. 0.0 and +1.0
    d. none of the above

37. In testing, extra-validity concerns refer to
   *a. unintended side effects of testing
    b. long-term validity effects
    c. content, criterion-related, and construct validity
    d. none of the above

38. The observation that almost all school systems report above average achievement scores is referred to as the
    a. self-fulfilling prophecy
   *b. Lake Wobegon Effect
    c. phantom correlation phenomenon
    d. none of the above

39. According to the functionalist perspective on test validity, a test is valid if
    a. inferences made from it are meaningful and appropriate
   *b. the test serves the purpose for which it is used
    c. its screening function is proved effective
    d. none of the above

Topic 4B

Test Construction

Defining the Test

Selecting a Scaling Method

    Levels of Measurement

Representative Scaling Methods

    Expert Rankings
    Method of Equal-Appearing Intervals
    Method of Absolute Scaling
    Likert Scales
    Guttman Scales
    Method of Empirical Keying
    Rational Scale Construction (Internal Consistency)

Constructing the Items

    Initial Questions in Test Construction
    Table of Specifications
    Item Formats

Testing the Items

    Item-Difficulty Index
    Item-Reliability Index
    Item-Validity Index
    Item-Characteristic Curves
    Item-Discrimination Index
    Reprise: The Best Items

Revising the Test

Cross-validation
Validity Shrinkage

Publishing the Test

Production of Testing Materials
Technical Manual and User's Manual
Testing is Big Business

Summary

Key Terms and Concepts

Classroom Discussion Questions

1. Students often find it difficult to comprehend the notion of levels of measurement. A useful way to approach this topic is through examples. The instructor and students can describe measurement methods and discuss the underlying levels of measurement. For example, the instructor can ask what level of measurement is involved in the following:

listing officers by rank
categorizing football players by position
describing storm conditions as gale force, hurricane, etc.
measuring electrodermal responsivity
assessing reaction time
calculating the weight of examinees
listing the social class (I-VI) of research subjects

2. This topic introduced several different formats for test items. Have students summarize these item types and discuss the advantages and disadvantages of each.

Extramural Assignments

1. An instructive assignment is to have students develop Likert and Guttman scales to measure various attributes. For example, students can develop a Likert attitude scale which assesses degree of formal religiosity; or a Guttman scale to assess level of depression. The most important point in this assignment is to illustrate the extreme difficulty in developing good scales.

2. Have students write up a table of specifications for your final examination. This assignment usually generates a lively discussion about the goals of education.

Classroom Demonstrations

1. Provide students with the necessary information to depict an item characteristic curve or to compute item-discrimination indices for your

test items. Have them portray these findings on the blackboard for general discussion.

2. If the instructors for your large introductory courses keep item information, bring in a computerized printout. Analyze specific questions and ask students for ways to improve "bad" items.

3. Most likely, you know a colleague who has developed a test or scale for research purposes. Invite him or her to class for a presentation on the nature and purpose of the scale.

Essay Questions

1. Define item analysis and describe its purpose(s).

2. Define cross-validation and discuss some of the general phenomena observed in cross-validation.

3. Give the formula for the item-discrimination index and define each of the terms. What values can the index take? What is a desirable value for the item-discrimination index?

4. What is meant by rational scale construction? What are its key characteristics?

5. Describe some ways in which an individual test can be made user-friendly.

TEST ITEM FILE

Topic 8: Test Construction

1. The first step in test construction is
    *a. defining the test
    b. selecting a scaling method
    c. constructing the items
    d. testing the items

2. Which of the below is a primary goal of the Kaufman Assessment Battery for Children?
    a. to measure intelligence from a strong theoretical and research basis
    b. to separate acquired factual knowledge from the ability to solve unfamiliar problems
    c. to yield scores that translate to educational intervention
    *d. all of the above

3. Which is the correct order for levels of measurement?
    a. ordinal, nominal, interval, ratio
    b. ordinal, nominal, ratio, interval
    c. nominal, ordinal, ratio, interval
    *d. nominal, ordinal, interval, ratio

4. In _____ scales, the numbers serve only as category names.
    *a. nominal
    b. ordinal
    c. interval
    d. ratio

5. A form of ranking is found in _____ scales.
    a. nominal
    *b. ordinal
    c. interval
    d. ratio

6. A(n) _____ scale has a conceptually meaningful zero point.
    a. nominal
    b. ordinal
    c. interval
    *d. ratio

7. The more powerful and useful statistics should only be used with _____ levels of measurement.
    a. nominal and ordinal
    b. ordinal and interval
    *c. interval and ratio
    d. ordinal and ratio

8. The Glasgow Coma Scale was developed by the method of
    a. factor analysis
    *b. expert rankings
    c. absolute scaling
    d. equal-appearing intervals

9. The method of equal-appearing intervals was developed by
    *a. Thurstone
    b. Likert
    c. Guttman
    d. Binet

10. The method of _____ involves ratings of favorability by expert judges.
    a. factor analysis
    b. expert rankings
    c. absolute scaling
    *d. equal-appearing intervals

11. In the method of _____, a set of common test items is administered to two or more age groups.
    a. factor analysis
    b. expert rankings
    *c. absolute scaling
    d. equal-appearing intervals

12. A _____ scale presents the examinee with five responses ordered on an agree/disagree or approve/disapprove continuum.
    a. Thurstone
  *b. Likert
    c. Guttman
    d. Binet

13. On a _____ scale, respondents who endorse one statement also agree with milder statements pertinent to the same underlying continuum.
    a. Thurstone
    b. Likert
  *c. Guttman
    d. Binet

14. The following items are probably an example of a _____ scale:
  ( ) I occasionally feel sad or blue.
  ( ) I often feel sad or blue.
  ( ) I feel sad or blue most of the time.
  ( ) I always feel sad and I can't stand it.
    a. Thurstone
    b. Likert
  *c. Guttman
    d. Binet

15. The method of _____ is entirely atheoretical.
  *a. empirical keying
    b. equal-appearing intervals
    c. absolute scaling
    d. expert rankings

16. Which scale construction method guarantees that all scale items correlate positively with each other and also with the total score for the scale?
    a. empirical keying
    b. equal-appearing intervals
  *c. rational scale construction
    d. expert rankings

17. A(n) _____ effect is observed when significant numbers of examinees obtain perfect or near-perfect scores.
    a. floor   c. interval
    *b. ceiling   d. absolute

18. It is common practice in test development that the prepublication version of a new instrument might contain _____ the number of items desired on the final draft.
    *a. fewer than
    b. double
    c. five times
    d. ten times

19. To help insure that a test contains the desired mixture of cognitive processes and content domains, test developers
    a. follow the guidelines specified by Binet
    b. use factor analysis on the test items
    *c. use a table of specifications
    d. always consult similar instruments before writing test items

20. For group-administered tests of intellect or achievement, the technique of choice is the
    a. short-answer essay
    b. true-false question
    *c. multiple choice question
    d. method of matching

21. From a psychometric standpoint, _____ questions are the weakest.
    a. multiple choice
    *b. matching
    c. true-false
    d. fill in the blank

22. For individually administered tests, the procedure of choice is the
    *a. short answer objective item
    b. multiple choice question
    c. open-ended question
    d. essay

23. The forced-choice methodology is designed to counter the problem of
   a. guessing
   *b. social desirability
   c. distractor difficulty
   d. all of the above

24. The proportion of examinees in a large tryout sample who get a specific item correct is called
   *a. item-difficulty index
   b. item-reliability index
   c. item-validity index
   d. index of item discrimination

25. The index of item difficulty can vary from
   a. 0 to 100
   b. -1.0 to +1.0
   *c. 0.0 to +1.0
   d. 0.5 to +1.0

26. In general, the optimal level of item difficulty is
   a. 0
   *b. .5
   c. 1.0
   d. 100

27. For true-false items, the optimal level of item difficulty is
   a. .5
   *b. .75
   c. 1.0
   d. 100

28. A test used to designate children for a remedial-education program should contain many _____ items.
   *a. extremely easy
   b. average difficulty
   c. moderately difficult
   d. extremely difficult

29. A dichotomously scored test item with good item reliability must
   a. have strong internal consistency
   b. produce a good dispersion of scores between its two alternatives
   *c. both a and b
   d. neither a nor b

30. To know how well each preliminary test item contributes to accurate prediction of the criterion, we would use
   a. item-difficulty index
   b. item-reliability index
   *c. item-validity index
   d. index of item discrimination

31. The point-biserial correlation between the item score and the score on the criterion variable is needed to compute the
   a. item-difficulty index
   b. item-reliability index
   *c. item-validity index
   d. index of item discrimination

32. A graphical display of the relationship between the probability of a correct response and the examinee's position on the underlying trait measured by the test is called
   a. item-difficulty index
   b. item-reliability index
   c. item-characteristic curve
   d. cumulative difficulty curve

33. The _____ is simply the normal distribution graphed in cumulative form.
   a. item-characteristic curve
   b. cumulative difficulty curve
   *c. normal ogive
   d. summative distribution

34. In order to investigate potential sex bias in a test item, we would examine a(n)
    *a. item-characteristic curve
    b. cumulative difficulty curve
    c. normal ogive
    d. summative distribution

35. The expression (U - L)/N defines the
    *a. item-discrimination index
    b. item-difficulty index
    c. item-characteristic curve
    d. cumulative difficulty curve

36. The item-discrimination index can vary from
    a. 0 to 100
    *b. -1.0 to +1.0
    c. 0.0 to +1.0
    d. 0.5 to +1.0

37. The optimal value for the item-discrimination index is
    a. 1.0
    b. 0.5
    c. 0.0
    d. 100

38. Suppose on we obtain the following response patterns on a multiple choice question with correct answer "c":

	a	b	c	d	e
high-scorers	5	6	80	5	4
low-scorers	15	14	40	16	15

What needs to be done to improve this test item?
    a. the overall difficulty should be decreased
    b. alternative c should be rewritten
    *c. nothing, this is a good test item
    d. the distractors should be made more difficult

39. Examinees used in a "tryout" sample should be _____ those for whom the test is ultimately intended.
   *a. highly similar to
   b. heterogeneous and different from
   c. homogeneous and different from
   d. younger than

40. The expression _____ refers to the practice of using the original regression equation in a new sample to determine if the test predicts the criterion as well as it did in the original sample.
   a. regression validation
   *b. cross-validation
   c. regression to the mean
   d. standardization

41. The expression _____ refers to the phenomenon in which a test predicts a criterion less well when used on a new sample of subjects.
   a. regression shrinkage
   b. regression to the mean
   c. validity reduction
   *d. validity shrinkage

42. Which of the following is a desirable feature for an individually administered test?
   a. putting the instructions on the answer sheet
   b. providing a standup ring binder for test materials
   c. using boldfaced type for the examiner's verbal instructions
   *d. all of the above

43. According to Arthur Jensen, the principal hindrances to psychometrically superior tests are
   a. copyright laws
   b. vested interests of test publishers
   c. the market economy for tests
   *d. all of the above

Topic 5A

Theories and the Measurement of Intelligence

Definitions of Intelligence

>Expert Definitions of Intelligence
>Layperson and Expert Conceptions of Intelligence

Case Exhibit 5.1: Learning and Adaptation as Core Functions of Intelligence

>Theories of Intelligence

>>Galton and Sensory Keenness
>>Spearman and the "g" Factor
>>Thurstone and the Primary Mental Abilities
>>R. Cattell and the Fluid/Crystallized Distinction
>>Piaget and Adaptation
>>Guilford and the Structure of Intellect Model
>>Theory of Simultaneous and Successive Processing
>>Intelligence as a Biological Construct
>>Gardner and the Theory of Multiple Intelligences
>>Sternberg and the Triarchic Theory of Intelligence

>Summary

>Key Terms and Concepts

Classroom Discussion Questions

1. A lively discussion is almost guaranteed if the instructor poses this question to students: What is intelligence? A useful approach is to write down student responses on the blackboard and search for commonalities, areas of agreement, and points of disagreement.

2. This topic presents the viewpoints of several different theorists. Although it is a difficult assignment, students can be challenged to pick a single theorist and justify why they prefer that viewpoint. This discussion question works best if assigned the previous class period.

3. Sternberg's theory is in many respects the most complex viewpoint presented in this topic. It is valuable to ask students to give examples of the various components of his theory.

Extramural Assignments

1. Replication is an essential component of modern research. Assign groups of students the task of replicating Sternberg's study on lay conceptions of intelligence (discussed in the text, Sternberg et al., 1981).

2. Guilford has proposed an elegant model of intelligence emphasizing five operations, five content areas, and six products. Assign students the task of devising instruments which are pure tests of a single component of intelligence (e.g., divergent production, symbolic content, and transformational products).

3. Jensen has emphasized that complex forms of reaction time are positively correlated with psychometric intelligence. Groups of students could conduct a simple correlational study, plotting and correlating reaction time versus cognitive skill. Several computer programs exist for measuring reaction time, whereas a short screening device such as the Shipley Institute of Living Scale can be used for the cognitive test.

Classroom Demonstrations

1. Before you present material from this chapter, ask students to write down brief descriptions of "intelligence." Then demonstrate for the students the parallels between their views and the findings of Sternberg et al. (1981) (discussed in the textbook).

2. Although the instructor must exercise care not to release the content of modern, copyrighted tests, it is always fascinating to provide students with sample items from discontinued or noncopyrighted tests. Students should be challenged to determine the underlying model of intelligence presupposed by the particular tests.

Essay Questions

1. Describe the major features of the Cattell-Horn model of intelligence.

2. Describe the major features of Gardner's model of intelligence.

3. Compare and contrast the Cattell-Horn and the Gardner models of intelligence.

4. What are the differences and similarities between lay and expert conceptions of intelligence?

TEST ITEM FILE

Topic 5A: Theories and the Measurement of Intelligence

1. A(n) _____ definition defines a concept in terms of the way it is measured.
   a. constructivist
   b. empirical
   c. real
   *d. operational

2. A(n) _____ definition is on that seeks to tell us the true nature of the thing being defined.
   a. constructivist
   b. empirical
   *c. real
   d. operational

3. "A general ability which involves mainly the eduction of relations and correlates" was the definition of intelligence offered by
   *a. Spearman
   b. Binet & Simon
   c. Wechsler
   d. Sternberg

4. "The ability to judge well, to understand well, to reason well" was the definition of intelligence offered by
   a. Spearman
   *b. Binet & Simon
   c. Wechsler
   d. Sternberg

5. "The mental capacity to automatize information processing and to emit contextually appropriate behavior in response to novelty" was the definition of intelligence offered by
   a. Spearman
   b. Binet & Simon
   c. Wechsler
   *d. Sternberg

6. "The aggregate or global capacity of the individual to act purposefully, to think rationally and to deal effectively with the environment" was the definition of intelligence offered by
    a. Spearman
    b. Binet & Simon
    *c. Wechsler
    d. Sternberg

7. Gardner (1986) defined intelligence as:
    *a. the ability or skill to solve problems or to fashion products which are valued within one or more cultural settings
    b. error-free transmission of information through the cortex
    c. the power of good responses from the point of view of truth or fact
    d. the capacity to form concepts and to grasp their significance

8. Broadly speaking, the experts tend to agree that intelligence is:
    a. the capacity to learn from experience
    b. the capacity to adapt to one's environment
    *c. both a and b
    d. neither a nor b

9. According to the textbook author, a possible problem with contemporary intelligence tests is that they do not
    a. emphasize verbal skills sufficiently
    b. incorporate culture-free perspectives in test items
    *c. require to subject to adapt to new situations
    d. none of the above

10. In order of importance, experts saw _____ as crucial to intelligence.
    *a. verbal intelligence, problem-solving ability, and practical intelligence
    b. problem-solving ability, practical intelligence, and verbal intelligence
    c. practical intelligence, problem-solving ability, and verbal intelligence
    d. practical intelligence, verbal intelligence, and problem-solving ability

11. Social competence as an ingredient of intelligence is emphasized by
    a. experts
    *b. laypersons
    c. both experts and laypersons
    d. neither experts nor laypersons

12. The "sensory keenness" approach to the measurement of intelligence
    a. died with Galton and Cattell
    *b. has modern proponents such as Jensen
    c. was discredited by Wechsler
    d. is exemplified by most modern instruments

13. Indices of reaction time correlate as high as ____ with traditional psychometric tests of intelligence.
    a. .20
    b. .50
    c. -.20
    *d. -.50

14. The analogy hammer:nail::screwdriver: ? exemplifies the approach to intelligence favored by
    a. Piaget
    b. Wechsler
    *c. Spearman
    d. Guilford

15. Spearman's theory of intelligence was
    a. derived from factor analysis
    b. physiological in emphasis
    c. based upon a single general factor
    *d. all of the above

16. The view that intelligence consists of about seven primary mental abilities was put forth by
    a. Wechsler
    b. Sternberg
    *c. Thurstone
    d. Guilford

17. Which of the following is a primary mental ability?
    a. verbal comprehension
    b. associative memory
    c. perceptual speed
    *d. all of the above

18. Vernon's two major group factors are
    *a. verbal-educational and practical-mechanical
    b. verbal-educational and practical-social
    c. verbal-social and practical-spatial
    d. verbal-social and practical-physical

19. A largely nonverbal and relatively culture-reduced form of mental efficiency is
    *a. fluid intelligence
    b. crystallized intelligence
    c. general intelligence
    d. spatial ability

20. What one has already learned through the investment of fluid intelligence in cultural settings is
    a. fluid intelligence
    *b. crystallized intelligence
    c. general intelligence
    d. spatial ability

21. The awareness that physical quantities do not change in amount when they are superficially altered in appearance is known as
    a. equilibration
    b. schema
    *c. conservation
    d. none of the above

22. An organized pattern of behavior or a well defined mental structure that leads to knowing how to do something:
    a. equilibration
    b. assimilation
    c. accomodation
    *d. schema

23. The application of a schema to an object, person, or event is
   a. equilibration
  *b. assimilation
   c. accommodation
   d. conservation

24. The adjustment of an unsuccessful schema so that it works is called
   a. equilibration
   b. assimilation
  *c. accommodation
   d. conservation

25. Compared to his predecessors, Guilford's approach to the study of intelligence placed a greater emphasis upon
   a. a large number of factors of intelligence
   b. the role of creativity in intelligence
   c. both a and b
  *d. neither a nor b

26. In Guilford's model, _____ refer to the nature of the materials or information presented to the examinee.
   a. operations
  *b. contents
   c. products
   d. factors

27. In Guilford's system, retrieving from memory items of a specific class, such as naming objects that are both hard and edible, is an example of
   a. convergent thinking
  *b. divergent thinking
   c. memory
   d. evaluation

28. In total, Guilford identified _____ factors of intellect.
   a. 50   *c. 150
   b. 100   d. 250

29. A test question such as "List as many consequences as possible if clouds had strings hanging down from them" is an index of
   a. convergent thinking
 *b. divergent thinking
   c. memory
   d. evaluation

30. The waveform of the average evoked potential has _____ peaks and troughs for high IQ subjects than for low IQ subjects.
   a. fewer
   b. the same number of
 *c. many more
   d. sharper

31. According to Gardner (1983), which of the following is a criterion for the existence of a separate intelligence?
   a. potential isolation by brain damage
   b. distinctive developmental history
   c. evolutionary plausibility
 *d. all of the above

32. Gardner has hypothesized that all of the following intelligences exist EXCEPT
   a. linguistic   c. bodily-kinesthetic
   b. musical   *d. intuitive

33. According to Gardner, personal intelligence is
   a. intrapersonal
   b. interpersonal
 *c. both a and b
   d. neither a nor b

34. A mentally deficient individual who has a highly developed talent in a single area is known as a(n)
 *a. idiot savant
   b. developmentally disabled person
   c. mentally deficient person
   d. none of the above

35. _____ intelligence consists of the internal mental mechanisms that are responsible for intelligent behavior.
    *a. Componential
    b. Experiential
    c. Contextual
    d. all of the above

36. According to Sternberg, a person with good _____ intelligence is able to deal effectively with novel tasks.
    a. componential
    *b. experiential
    c. contextual
    d. fluid

37. _____ intelligence is defined as mental activity involved in purposive adaptation to, shaping of, and selection of real-world environments relevant to one's life.
    a. Componential
    b. Experiential
    *c. Contextual
    d. all of the above

38. According to Sternberg, the ability to leave the environment we are in and to find a different environment more suitable to our talents and needs is known as
    *a. selection
    b. meta-cognition
    c. componential reasoning
    d. adaptation

Topic 5B

Assessment of Infant and Preschool Abilities

Assessment of Infant Abilities

    Gesell Developmental Schedules
    Denver Developmental Screening Test-Revised
    Ordinal Scales of Psychological Development
    Bayley Scales of Infant Development-II
    In Brief: Additional Measures of Infant Ability

Assessment of Preschool Intelligence

    The Wechsler Preschool and Primary Scale of Intelligence-Revised (WPPSI-R)
    WPPSI-R Subtests
    Stanford-Binet: Fourth Edition
    Kaufman Assessment Battery for Children (K-ABC)
    McCarthy Scales of Children's Abilities
    Differential Ability Scales

Practical Utility of Infant and Preschool Assessment

    Predictive Validity of Infant and Preschool Tests
    Practical Utility of the Bayley-II and Other Infant Scales
    New Approaches to Infant Assessment

Summary

Classroom Discussion Questions

1. Ask students to brainstorm on the possible approaches to assessment of infant intelligence. What kinds of tests could be used? What kinds of items would they incorporate? The instructor might make a list on the blackboard as the discussion proceeds. A natural followup is to compare the students' ideas with the actual content of tests such as the Bayley Scales of Infant Development.

2. One point made in this topic is that intelligence possesses minimal stability from infancy to preschool to early childhood. Ask students to discuss the reasons for this instability.

Extramural Assignments

1. Ask students to observe infants under one year of age and describe the evidences of intelligence. For example, what kinds of problems can a six-month-old infant solve? What are the sensori-motor capabilities of a three-month-old infant? And so on.

Classroom Demonstrations

1. If the instructor has access to infant tests, a useful classroom activity is to demonstrate the test with infants volunteered by students or others.

2. Arrange for a specialist to discuss procedures for the evaluation of infants at risk for mental retardation. For example, many population centers have federally-funded Child Development Centers which employ educational specialists. Ask one of the specialists to speak to the class.

Essay Questions

1. What is the practical utility of the Bayley-II and other infant scales?

2. Discuss recent, innovative approaches to the assessment of infant intelligence.

TEST ITEM FILE

Topic 5B: Assessment of Infant and Preschool Abilities

1. The first infant test was the
   - *a. Gesell Developmental Schedules
   - b. Denver Developmental Screening Test
   - c. Hunt-Uzgiris Scales
   - d. Bayley Scales of Infant Development

2. For well-trained observers, the inter-observer reliability of the Gesell Developmental Schedules is in the
   - a. .60s
   - b. .70s
   - c. .80s
   - *d. .90s

3. Significant delay in meeting the developmental milestones of the Gesell Developmental Schedules may indicate
   - a. neurological impairment
   - b. mental retardation
   - *c. both a and b
   - d. neither a nor b

4. The most widely known and researched pediatric screening tool in the United States is probably the
   - a. Gesell Developmental Schedules
   - *b. Denver Developmental Screening Test
   - c. Ordinal Scales of Psychological Development
   - d. Bayley Scales of Infant Development

5. The Denver Developmental Screening Test provides assessment in the following domain(s):
   - a. language
   - b. personal-social
   - c. fine motor-adaptive
   - *d. all of the above

6. A review of five studies using the Denver Developmental Screening Test indicated that, on average, about _____ percent of those identified as abnormal by the DDST later turn out to be developmentally normal.
    *a. 5
    b. 10
    c. 15
    d. 20

7. The Denver Developmental Screening Test fails to detect about _____ of infants who later show a poor outcome.
    a. 20
    b. 40
    c. 60
    *d. 80

8. The Ordinal Scales of Psychological Development are based upon the work of
    a. Binet   c. Bayley
    *b. Piaget   d. Terman

9. The Bayley Scales of Infant Development-II consists of the following scale(s)
    a. mental scale
    b. motor scale
    c. behavior rating scale
    *d. all of the above

10. For technical quality and standardization, the best infant test is probably the
    a. Gesell Developmental Schedules
    b. Denver Developmental Screening Test
    c. Ordinal Scales of Psychological Development
    *d. Bayley Scales of Infant Development-II

11. The age range for the Bayley Scales of Infant Development-II is
    *a. 1 to 42 months
    b. 2 to 60 months
    c. 6 to 60 months
    d. 6 to 120 months

12. Comparing the Bayley Scales of Infant Development-II and the Denver Developmental Screening Test,
    a. the Bayley takes more skill to administer
    b. the Bayley takes longer to administer
    *c. both a and b
    d. neither a nor b

13. Regarding the predictive value of infant tests,
    a. when scores are near normal or higher, the tests possess little or no predictive validity
    b. for infants who score in the lowest few percentiles, infant tests validly predict a handicapped outcome in childhood
    *c. both a and b
    d. neither a nor b

14. In an attempt to improve predictive validity, the most recent infant tests have assessed
    a. brain waves
    b. Piagetian skills
    *c. visual habituation
    d. none of the above

15. Which is the most modern infant test?
    a. Denver Developmental Screening Test
    b. Hunt-Uzgiris Scales
    c. Bayley Scales of Infant Development
    *d. Fagan's Test of Infant Intelligence

16. The SB:FE contains a total of _____ subtests.
    a. 5   *c. 15
    b. 10   d. none of the above

17. The _____ emphasizes memory skills to a far greater extent than any other test of general intelligence.
    a. WAIS-R
    b. McCarthy Scales of Children's Ability
    c. Slosson Intelligence Test
    *d. Stanford-Binet: Fourth Edition

18. The SB:FE produces ____ area scores
    a. one
    b. two
    c. three
    *d. four

19. The K-ABC is designed to assess
    a. intelligence
    b. achievement
    c. personality
    d. both a and b

20. The age range for the K-ABC is approximately
    *a. 2 through 12
    b. 6 through 16
    c. 2 through 18
    d. 6 through adulthood

21. The two major subscales of the K-ABC are
    a. verbal and performance
    b. verbal and perceptual-motor
    *c. simultaneous and sequential
    d. simultaneous and gestalt

22. An important goal of the K-ABC is to
    *a. provide scores that translate to educational intervention
    b. diagnose attention-deficit hyperactivity disorder
    c. select children for gifted and talented programs
    d. assess the general factor in intelligence

23. On the K-ABC, differences in overall score between white and minority samples tend to be on the order of ____ points.
    *a. 5
    b. 10
    c. 15
    d. 20

24. The K-ABC includes the following scale(s)
    a. Achievement
    b. Nonverbal
    *c. both a and b
    d. neither a nor b

25. Correlations between K-ABC scores and measures of childhood anxiety are
    a. strong and positive
    b. strong and negative
    *c. negligible
    d. unknown

26. The correlation between WISC-R IQ and K-ABC Composite score is about
    a. .2
    b. .4
    c. .6
    *d. .8

27. The achievement tests on the K-ABC
    a. closely resemble traditional measures of intelligence
    b. have strong loadings on a general factor of intelligence
    *c. both a and b
    d. neither a nor b

28. The approximate age range for the McCarthy Scales of Children's Abilities is
    *a. 2 1/2 to 8 1/2
    b. 2 1/2 to 12 1/2
    c. 2 1/2 to 16 1/2
    d. 5 1/2 to 15 1/2

29. The choice of content for the McCarthy Scales of Children's Abilities was based upon
    a. factor analysis
    b. earlier children's tests
    *c. the test author's experience
    d. none of the above

30. The McCarthy Scales of Children's Abilities consists of ___ separate subscales.
    a. 6   *c. 18
    b. 12   d. 24

31. The General Cognitive Index from the McCarthy Scales of Children's Abilities underestimates IQs of
    *a. learning disabled and retarded children
    b. normal and near-normal children
    c. both a and b
    d. neither a nor b

32. In predicting scholastic achievement in the sixth grade from kindergarten results on the McCarthy Scales of Children's Abilities, which scale works best?
    *a. Quantitative Scale
    b. Verbal Scale
    c. Quantitative and Verbal Scales work equally well
    d. none of the above

33. A major objective with the Differential Ability Scales was to
    a. achieve highly reliable subtests
    b. produce homogeneous subtests
    *c. both a and b
    d. neither a nor b

34. In structure and purpose, this subtest is similar to Digit Span, but is designed to be more meaningful to the young examinees for whom it is intended.
    a. Mazes
    b. Coding
    *c. Sentences
    d. Animal Pegs

35. The Geometric Design subtest is included on which Wechsler Test(s)?
    *a. WPPSI-R   c. WISC-R
    b. WAIS-R   d. all of the above

36. Which instrument is a good tool for the diagnosis of mild to severe mental retardation in young children?
   a. WISC-R
   *b. WPPSI-R
   c. WAIS-R
   d. all of the above

Topic 6A

Individual Tests of Intelligence

Orientation to Individual Intelligence Tests

The Wechsler Scales of Intelligence

The Wechsler Subtests: Description and Analysis

Wechsler Adult Intelligence Scale-Revised

Wechsler Intelligence Scale for Children-III

Stanford-Binet Intelligence Scale: Fourth Edition

Detroit Tests of Learning Aptitude-3

Kaufman Brief Intelligence Test (K-BIT)

Summary

Key Terms and Concepts

Classroom Discussion Questions

1. Wechsler started with the axiomatic assumption that IQ does not show any systematic change with age. Based upon this assumption, the average IQ at any age is always 100. Is this a reasonable assumption?

2. The subtests of the Wechsler scales are well accepted as indices of intelligence. It may prove interesting to ask students their opinion of the subtests as measures of intelligence. Can they nominate other types of items for a Wechsler-type intelligence test?

3. Over half of the Wechsler subtests have strict time limits and/or bonus points for quick performance. Should an intelligence test incorporate such aspects of speed?

4. One point made in this topic is that vocabulary often emerges as an excellent measure of intelligence. This is a seemingly counterintuitive finding, since most people regard vocabulary as merely an index of schooling. Ask students to speculate upon why vocabulary almost invariably turns out to be a valuable component of individual intelligence tests.

5. Occasionally, the media will report that some famous personage, past or present, has a phenomenal IQ of 200 or above. Have students discuss their reactions to these reports. Would such a person be capable of greater accomplishments than a person with a "mere" 140 IQ. Point out to the students that existing individual IQ tests top out at around 164.

Extramural Assignments

1. If students have access to a major library, an interesting assignment is to ask them to trace the roots of the Wechsler subtests and items. Students are usually surprised to learn the extent to which Wechsler relied upon his predecessors. An excellent resource in this regard is Yerkes, R. M. (Ed.) (1921). Psychological examining in the United States army. Memoirs of the National Academy of Sciences, Volume 15.

2. The Wechsler scales are used for numerous applications in clinical psychology, medical psychology, neuropsychology, and related fields. Ask students to find research articles which make use of the Wechsler scales. What are the findings? How do the findings bear upon the utility of the Wechsler scales?

3. Have students summarize validity studies on the major individual intelligence tests (Wechsler scales, SB:FE, K-ABC, K-BIT, etc). These studies can be found in the Journal of Psychoeducational Assessment, and the Journal of Clinical Psychology, among others. To what extent do recent studies continue to support the validity of these instruments?

Classroom Demonstrations

1. Invite a practicing clinical psychologist or neuropsychologist to class to discuss the value of the Wechsler scales in assessment and diagnosis. If possible, have this person bring in profile scores and talk about the various subtests as they relate to individual assessment.

2. After obtaining appropriate informed consent, ask a psychologist to administer portions of the Wechsler Preschool and Primary Scale of Intelligence-Revised or Wechsler Intelligence Scale-III to a child. Leave time so students can ask questions about the nature of the test administration.

Essay Questions

1. Discuss the factorial structure of the Wechsler scales.

2. List and describe at least four Wechsler verbal scales and four performance scales.

3. Describe appropriate precautions in the administration of the Digit Span subtest from the Wechsler scales.

4. Which of the Wechsler subtests can be considered "weak" and in what sense can they be so considered?

5. Describe the cognitive abilities factors of the Stanford-Binet: Fourth Edition.

TEST ITEM FILE

Topic 6A: Individual Tests of Intelligence

1. Next to Binet and Simon, the one individual who has had the greatest influence upon the testing of individual intelligence is
    a. Terman
    b. Guilford
    *c. Wechsler
    d. Thurstone

2. In developing his intelligence tests, Wechsler
    a. was an innovator who invented many new subtests
    b. used old subtests and newly created subtests in about equal number
    *c. borrowed heavily from existing instruments for most subtests
    d. started from scratch with a completely new conception of intelligence

3. The first Wechsler test was the _____, designed for the assessment of _____
    *a. Wechsler-Bellevue, adults
    b. Wechsler-Bellevue, children
    c. Wechsler Intelligence Scale, children
    d. Wechsler Intelligence Scale, adults

4. Wechsler's first intelligence test was based upon the assumption(s) that
    a. IQ remains constant with normal aging
    b. raw intellectual ability may decline with age
    *c. both a and b
    d. neither a nor b

5. Which formula(s) depict how Wechsler computed IQs?
    a. IQ = mental age/chronological age
    *b. IQ = attained score/expected mean score for age
    c. both a and b
    d. neither a nor b

6. Wechsler's purpose in dividing his scales into verbal and performance sections was to use his test in
   a. hemispheric lateralization
   b. educational assessment
   c. vocational guidance
   *d. psychiatric diagnosis

7. Wechsler believed that the following condition(s) gave rise to a test pattern of verbal greater than performance IQ:
   a. organic brain disease
   b. psychoses
   c. emotional disorders
   *d. all of the above

8. Typically, the Wechsler tests contain how many subtests?
   a. 2
   b. 5-6
   *c. 10-12
   d. 15

9. For the Wechsler tests, the standard deviation of IQ is always
   a. 5   *c. 15
   b. 10   d. 20

10. Wechsler defined intelligence as
   *a. the aggregate or global capacity of the individual to act purposefully, to think rationally and to deal effectively with his environment
   b. the ability to judge well, to act well, and to reason well
   c. high level reasoning in the service of everyday life
   d. the ability to solve problems or fashion solutions that are valued in one or more cultural contexts

11. Factual knowledge of persons, places, and common phenomena is tested by the _____ subtest.
   a. Comprehension
   b. Similarities
   c. Picture Completion
   *d. Information

12. The _____ subtest has the highest correlation with overall IQ.
    a. Comprehension
    b. Similarities
    *c. Vocabulary
    d. Information

13. Indirectly, this subtest measures learning and memory skills insofar as subjects must retain knowledge gained from formal and informal educational opportunities in order to answer the items.
    a. Comprehension
    b. Similarities
    c. Vocabulary
    *d. Information

14. Performance on this subtest may be affected by anxiety or fatigue, and many clinicians have noted that patients hospitalized for medical or psychiatric reasons frequently perform poorly on it.
    a. Vocabulary
    *b. Digit Span
    c. Picture Completion
    d. Comprehension

15. In _____ the examinee must form an internal visual mental trace in order to answer the items correctly.
    a. Digits Forward
    *b. Digits Backward
    c. both a and b
    d. neither a nor b

16. Performance on this subtest is dependent upon the lifelong application of contextual inference.
    a. Block Design   c. Digit Symbol
    b. Information   *d. Vocabulary

17. Which of the following subtests has a time limit?
    *a. Arithmetic   c. Vocabulary
    b. Vocabulary   d. Similarities

18. In factor analyses of the Wechsler tests, this subtest frequently loads on a third factor variously interpreted as "freedom from distractibility" or "memory."
   *a. Arithmetic
   b. Vocabulary
   c. Comprehension
   d. Similarities

19. On the WAIS-R, this subtest requires the examinee to interpret proverbs.
   a. Picture Arrangement
   b. Vocabulary
   *c. Comprehension
   d. Similarities

20. More than anywhere else in the WAIS-R, this subtest allows for the observation of the client's natural thought processes and cognitive problem-solving style.
   a. Picture Arrangement
   b. Vocabulary
   *c. Comprehension
   d. Similarities

21. This subtest evaluates the examinee's ability to distinguish important from unimportant resemblances in objects, facts, and ideas.
   a. Picture Arrangement
   b. Vocabulary
   c. Comprehension
   *d. Similarities

22. This subtest consistently demonstrates resilience to the effects of brain damage.
   a. Block Design
   *b. Picture Completion
   c. Digit Span
   d. Digit Symbol

23. On this subtest, the more difficult items require the analysis of spatial relations, visual-motor coordination, and the rigid application of logic.
    *a. Block Design
    b. Picture Completion
    c. Digit Span
    d. Digit Symbol

24. In general, this subtest has the highest correlation with Performance IQ.
    *a. Block Design
    b. Picture Completion
    c. Digit Span
    d. Digit Symbol

25. The _____ factor of the Wechsler tests is variously identified as nonverbal, visuospatial, or perceptual-organizational intelligence.
    a. first
    *b. second
    c. third
    d. fourth

26. This subtest is strongly speeded, that is, adults must perform very quickly to get maximum scores.
    *a. Block Design
    b. Vocabulary
    c. Comprehension
    d. Similarities

27. This subtest is the least reliable of the Wechsler subtests.
    a. Block Design
    b. Picture Completion
    *c. Object Assembly
    d. Vocabulary

28. Efficient performance on this subtest requires the ability to quickly produce distinctive verbal codes to represent symbols in memory.
    a. Block Design
    b. Picture Completion
    c. Digit Span
    *d. Digit Symbol

29. Performance on this subtest shows a steep decrement with advancing age.
   a. Vocabulary
   b. Comprehension
   c. Picture Completion
   *d. Digit Symbol

30. This subtest is one of the most sensitive subtests to the effects of organic impairment.
   a. Vocabulary
   b. Comprehension
   c. Similarities
   *d. Digit Symbol

31. This subtest is a poor measure of general intelligence, but measures perceptual organization reasonably well.
   a. Vocabulary
   b. Block Design
   *c. Mazes
   d. Information

32. The WAIS-R contains about ____ percent of the items from the WAIS.
   a. 20
   b. 40
   c. 60
   *d. 80

33. For a typical short form of the WAIS-R, the estimated IQ will be within ____ points of the actual IQ about two-thirds of the time.
   a. 4
   *b. 9
   c. 14
   d. 19

34. The standardization sample of the WAIS-R was carefully stratified on
   a. race
   b. geographic region
   c. educational attainment
   *d. all of the above

35. The standardization sample of the WAIS-R shows pecularities in which age group?
    *a. 16-17
    b. 25-29
    c. 40-49
    d. 60-69

36. In general, WAIS-R IQs are _____ WAIS IQs.
    a. much higher than
    b. slightly higher than
    *c. lower than
    d. about the same as

37. The split-half reliability of WAIS-R Full Scale IQ is about
    a. .67
    b. .77
    c. .87
    *d. .97

38. For WAIS-R IQ, the standard error of measurement is about
    *a. 2.5
    b. 5.0
    c. 7.5
    d. 10.0

39. The correlation between WAIS-R and Stanford-Binet IQs is about
    a. .6
    b. .7
    c. .8
    *d. .9

40. WAIS-R verbal tests tend to tap _____ intelligence; performance tests tend to tap _____ intelligence.
    a. crystallized, crystallized
    *b. crystallized, fluid
    c. fluid, fluid
    d. fluid, crystallized

41. Which test(s) used African-Americans in the standardization
sample?   a. WISC and WISC-R
              b. WISC only
             *c. WISC-R only
              d. neither WISC nor WISC-R

42. On the WISC-R, which subtest(s) load on the perceptual
organization factor?
       a. Picture Completion
       b. Picture Arrangement
       c. Block Design
      *d. all of the above

43. In general, it appears that normative data for the SB:FE are
_____ the target population.
      *a. quite representative of
       b. unrepresentative of
       c. of unknown relationship to
       d. none of the above

44. The test-retest reliability of the SB:FE subtests is
       a. consistently in the .90s
      *b. quite variable, ranging from the high .20s to the .70s
       c. unknown, since the test developers used KR-20 estimates
       d. consistently in the .70s

45. On the SB:FE, the _____ subtest is used as a routing
test for the remainder of the examination.
       a. Comprehension   c. Matrices
      *b. Vocabulary   d. Verbal Relations

46. Conceptually, on the SB:FE the basal level is the level
       a. typically passed by examinees of that age
       b. consists of those subtests typically passed by examinees
who are two years younger than the examinee
      *c. below which, the examinee would almost certainly answer all
questions correctly
       d. none of the above

47. In general, confirmatory factor analysis studies of the SB:FE provide _____ support for the existence of the four factors posited in the construction of the test.
   a. no
   *b. weak
   c. strong
   d. extremely strong

48. The most serious problem with the SB:FE is
   a. absence of criterion validity
   b. absence of simple items for mildly retarded persons
   *c. nonuniformity of composite scores
   d. none of the above

49. The most serious problem with the DTLA-3 is that
   a. the test is not a good measure of general intelligence
   b. the norms are based upon too few subjects
   *c. the breakdown into composites is not empirically supported
   d. none of the above

50. The KBIT consists of two parts:
   *a. Vocabulary and Matrices
   b. Verbal and Performance
   c. Vocabulary and Performance
   d. Verbal and Matrices

51. Evidence for reliability and validity of the KBIT can be characterized as:
   a. nonexistent
   b. weak
   c. moderate
   *d. strong

Topic 6B

Group Tests of Intelligence

Origins and Characteristics of Group Tests

Multidimensional Aptitude Battery (MAB)

Background and Description
Technical Features
Comment on the MAB

Shipley Institute of Living Scale (SILS)

Background and Description
Technical Features
Comment on the SILS

A Multilevel Battery: The Cognitive Abilities Test (CogAT)

Background and Description
Technical Features
Comment on the CogAT

Culture Fair Intelligence Test (CFIT)

Background and Description
Technical Features
Comment on the CFIT

Raven's Progressive Matrices (RPM)

Background and Description
Technical Features
Comment on the RPM

Perspective on Culture-Fair Tests

Summary

Key Terms and Concepts

Classroom Discussion Questions

1. This topic can be introduced with a general discussion of the differences between group and individual intelligence tests, as well as the advantages and disadvantages of each. A useful approach is for the instructor to make a list on the blackboard as the discussion proceeds.

2. This question usually arouses passionate views in students: What would be the characteristics of a culture-free intelligence test? Is good intelligence the same in all cultures or is it relative to each specific culture?

3. As noted in the first chapter, the pioneers of testing regarded performance tests as the best index of culture-free (or at least culture-reduced) intelligence. Demonstrate the materials for various performance tests. Then have the students discuss to what extent these tests are culture-laden. It is worth pointing out that even the concept of taking a test is culture-loaded.

Extramural Assignments

1. Many popular paperbacks claim to provide a self-measure of IQ. Have students purchase one or two of these books and write an analysis of the tests contained within them. What kinds of questions do these tests contain? To what extent do the authors provide norms? To what extent have the tests been subjected to any form of reliability or validity study?

2. Encourage students to learn about Mensa. Have them determine what kind of tests Mensa uses to qualify members. Then ask them to write an essay on the pros and cons of belonging to such an organization. Is it always socially useful to glorify high intelligence?

123

Classroom Demonstrations

1. Invite a public school administrator to speak about the use of group intelligence tests in his or her school system. Which tests are used? On what basis were the tests selected?

2. Purchase a "Know your IQ" type of book from a bookstore. Administer the test in class and have students self-score the test. Ask students to discuss the fairness and adequacy of the instrument. Be sure to point out whether the instrument was ever properly standardized.

Essay Questions

1. Compare and contrast the advantages and disadvantages of individual and group intelligence tests.

2. Describe the nature of the test items for these tests: Multidimensional Aptitude Battery (MAB), Raven's Progressive Matrices (RPM), and Shipley Institute of Living Scale (SILS).

3. Describe the Culture Fair Intelligence Test (CFIT) and discuss whether it is truly a culture fair measure of intelligence.

TEST ITEM FILE

Topic 6B: Group Tests of

Do you want "group" IQ?

1. The modern group intelligence test can be traced back to
   a. Wundt's laboratory studies of reaction time
   b. Galton's laboratory studies of sensory perception
   *c. Ebbinghaus's completion technique
   d. Cattell's sensory test battery

2. Which of the following is a feature that generally distinguishes a group test from an individual test of intelligence?
   a. multiple choice format
   b. used for screening
   c. huge standardization samples
   *d. all of the above

3. Group tests may not be the best choice for subjects who are
   a. shy
   b. confused
   c. unmotivated
   *d. all of the above

4. The risk in group testing is that some examinees will
   *a. score far below their true ability
   b. find the test to be too difficult
   c. object to being tested in the presence of other examinees
   d. none of the above

5. The Multidimensional Aptitude Battery is designed to be a paper-and-pencil equivalent of the
   a. SB:FE
   *b. WAIS-R
   c. K-ABC
   d. Differential Aptitude Test

6. The format for the Multidimensional Aptitude Battery is
   *a. multiple choice
   b. true-false
   c. short-answer objective items
   d. none of the above

7. The Multidimensional Aptitude Battery does not have a
   _____ subtest.
   a. Similarities
   b. Object Assembly
   c. Digit Symbol
   *d. Block Design

8. Which of the following is a subtest from the Multidimensional Aptitude Battery?
    a. Absurdities
    *b. Spatial
    c. Geometric Design
    d. Digit Span

9. The subtests from the Multidimensional Aptitude Battery incorporate
    a. power
    b. speed
    *c. both a and b
    d. neither a nor b

10. Including instructions, the Multidimensional Aptitude Battery takes about _____ minutes to administer
    a. 25   c. 75
    *b. 50   d. 100

11. Which standardization strategy did the developers of the Multidimensional Aptitude Battery employ?
    a. they used large, representative, stratified samples
    *b. they calibrated test scores to the WAIS-R as an anchor test
    c. both a and b
    d. neither a nor b

12. The correlation coefficients between Multidimensional Aptitude Battery and WAIS-R IQs were found to be about ___, ___, and ___, for Verbal, Performance, and Full Scale IQ, respectively.
    a. .7, .8, .9
    b. .7, .9, .8
    c. .8, .9, .7
    *d. .8, .7, .9

13. The internal consistency reliability of Multidimensional Aptitude Battery IQs is generally in the ___.
    a. .60s
    b. .70s
    c. .80s
    *d. .90s

14. Factor analyses of the Multidimensional Aptitude Battery reveal ___ factors identifiable as _____.
    *a. 2, verbal and performance
    b. 2, verbal and motor speed
    c. 3, verbal, performance, and attention
    d. 3, verbal, motor speed, and attention

15. The most difficult verbal items on the Multidimensional Aptitude Battery require a _____ grade reading level.
    a. fourth   c. eighth
    b. sixth   *d. tenth

16. The Culture Fair Intelligence Test was first conceived in the _____.
                    *a. 1920s
                     b. 1940s
                     c. 1960s
                     d. 1980s

17. The test manual for the Culture Fair Intelligence Test makes what recommendation with respect to Forms A and B.
    a. since the forms are equivalent, the tester can use either one
    b. the tester should use Form A first, saving Form B for a retest if needed
    *c. the tester should use both Form A and Form B together
    d. none of the above

18. The Culture Fair Intelligence Test is
    *a. a good measure of general intelligence
    b. a culture free measure of intelligence
    c. both a and b
    d. neither a nor b

19. Correlations between the Culture Fair Intelligence Test and other mainstream instruments such as the Wechsler Scales or the Stanford-Binet are generally in the _____.
    a. .30s
    b. .50s
    *c. .70s
    d. .90s

20. Raven's Progressive Matrices was originally designed as a measure of
   a. culture-free intelligence
   *b. Spearman's g factor
   c. crystallized intelligence
   d. none of the above

21. For adults with superior intelligence, the preferred test is
   a. Coloured Progressive Matrices
   b. Standard Progressive Matrices
   *c. Advanced Progressive Matrices
   d. Phase III Progressive Matrices

22. For the Standard Progressive Matrices, a typical split-half reliability is about
   a. .55
   b. .65
   c. .75
   *d. .85

23. Regarding the correlation between Raven's Progressive Matrices and other measures
   a. the correlations are higher for verbal tests
   *b. the correlations are higher for performance tests
   c. there is little difference in the correlations with verbal and performance tests
   d. in general, the average correlation hovers near zero for both verbal and performance tests

24. Which test is particularly valuable for the supplemental testing of children and adults with hearing, language, or physical disabilities?
   a. Multidimensional Aptitude Battery
   b. Shipley Institute of Living Scale
   c. Cognitive Abilities Test
   *d. Raven's Progressive Matrices

25. The original purpose of the Shipley Institute of Living Scale was to provide a measure of
    a. nonverbal intelligence
    b. culture-free intelligence
    *c. intellectual deterioration
    d. none of the above

26. The Shipley Institute of Living Scale is a(n)
    a. life skills achievement test
    *b. screening test of general intelligence
    c. index of adaptive behavior
    d. all of the above

27. Most examiners consider the Shipley Institute of Living Scale to be a
    *a. power test
    b. speed test
    c. speed and power test
    d. none of the above

28. On the vocabulary section of the Shipley Institute of Living Scale,
    *a. points are added for unanswered items
    b. points are subtracted for incorrect answers
    c. both a and b
    d. neither a nor b

29. Based upon the Shipley Institute of Living Scale, the correct answer to the progression below is _____
    135 341 52 12__
    *a. 3
    b. 4
    c. 5
    d. 6

30. On the Shipley Institute of Living Scale, the predicted score is derived from a regression equation that uses
    a. Vocabulary score
    b. age
    c. educational level
    *d. all of the above

31. Odd-even reliability estimates for the Shipley Institute of Living Scale tend to be about
    a. .6
    b. .7
    c. .8
    *d. .9

32. The 95 percent confidence interval for IQs estimated from the Shipley Institute of Living Scale is about plus or minus ___ points.
    a. 5   *c. 11
    b. 8   d. 14

33. On the Shipley Institute of Living Scale, old age tends to affect which score(s)?
    *a. mainly abstractions
    b. mainly vocabulary
    c. both abstractions and vocabulary
    d. neither abstractions nor vocabulary

34. The test manual norms on the Shipley Institute of Living Scale are based upon
    a. normal subjects
    *b. psychiatric subjects
    c. both a and b
    d. neither a nor b

35. The Shipley Institute of Living Scale is probably inappropriate for persons with
    a. low IQs
    b. language handicaps
    *c. both a and b
    d. neither a nor b

36. The subtests of the Cognitive Abilities Test are grouped into ___ batteries consisting of _____ tests.
    a. 2, verbal and quantitative
    b. 2, verbal and nonverbal
    *c. 3, verbal, quantitative, and nonverbal
    d. 3, verbal, perceptual, and nonverbal

37. The Cognitive Abilities Test resembles the
    a. Wechsler Intelligence Scale for Children-Revised
    *b. Stanford-Binet: Fourth Edition
    c. Kaufman Assessment Battery for Children
    d. none of the above

38. The Cognitive Abilities Test was standardized concurrently with
    a. the Iowa Tests of Basic Skills
    b. the Tests of Achievement and Proficiency
    *c. both a and b
    d. neither a nor b

39. Regarding ethnic differences on the Cognitive Abilities Test, the test authors
    *a. tried to minimize them during test development
    b. paid no attention to them during test development
    c. discovered that ethnic differences were minimal
    d. none of the above

40. Correlations between the Cognitive Abilities Test and the Stanford-Binet tend to be around
    a. .1
    b. .3
    c. .5
    *d. .7

41. On the Cognitive Abilities Test, correlations among the verbal, quantitative, and nonverbal batteries are in the
    a. .30s
    b. .50s
    *c. .70s
    d. .90s

42. Which of the following is NOT a school-based group intelligence test?
    a. Otis-Lennon School Ability Test
    b. School and College Ability Tests
    c. Kuhlman-Anderson
    *d. Kaufman Group Ability Test

Topic 7A:

Testing Special Populations

Origins of Tests for Special Populations
    Approaches to Assessment of Special Populations

The Legal Mandate for Assessing Persons with Disabilities

    Public Law 94-142
    Public Law 99-457
    Americans with Disabilities Act

Nonlanguage Tests

    Leiter International Performance Scale
    Human-Figure-Drawing Tests
    Hiskey-Nebraska Test of Learning Aptitude
    Test of Nonverbal Intelligence-2

Nonreading and Motor-Reduced Tests

Case Exhibit 7.1: The Challenge of Assessment in Cerebral Palsy

    Peabody Picture Vocabulary Test-Revised
    Columbia Mental Maturity Scale

Tests for Visually-Impaired Persons

Assessment of Adaptive Behavior in Mental Retardation

    Definition of Mental Retardation
    Scales of Independent Behavior
    Independent Living Behavior Checklist (ILBC)
    Additional Measures of Adaptive Behavior

Summary

Key Terms and Concepts

Classroom Discussion Questions

1. Some students have friends or siblings who qualified for services under Public Law 94-142. With permission, discuss the nature of these services, how the recipient and parents felt about the procedures, etc.

2. Some students know persons or have siblings who are developmentally disabled. With permission, discuss the nature of assessments conducted with these persons. Did the assessment services seem appropriate and helpful?

3. Have students list and discuss all the provisions of Public Law 94-142. Discuss what impacts this law has had upon assessment practices with handicapped persons.

Extramural Assignments

1. Although it would be unwieldy to have the entire class do this, some students could interview local school psychologists as to types of tests used with disabled children, perceptions about Public Law 94-142, and the like. The students could write a report or deliver a talk to the class.

2. Request that students consult Mental Measurements Yearbook or the Test Critiques series to find additional tests for disabled persons. Have them write a short report or deliver a talk to the class on the nature and psychometric characteristics of these instruments.

3. The textbook includes sufficient information for students to obtain raw scores for a draw-a-person test. Have groups of students obtain draw-a-person protocols from children of different ages to determine the relationship between age and raw scores.
Classroom Demonstrations

4. Students could simulate the effects of various disabilities and take sample tests of various types. For example, those with eyeglasses could spread Vaseline over their lenses and attempt a visual test (e.g.,

Digit Symbol). Other students could put in ear plugs and take an auditory test (e.g., Digit Span).

5. Sample draw-a-person protocols for children of various ages could be brought to class and scored according to the criteria listed in the textbook. Scores could be compared to ages. The adequacy of the criteria could be discussed.

6. Many of the instruments in this topic could be demonstrated to the class without concern for violation of professional ethics. For example, the Scales of Independent Behavior could be shown to the class, and simulated items from the Peabody Picture Vocabulary Test-Revised could be demonstrated without fear of revealing test-item content.

Essay Questions

1. Define the criteria for mental retardation.

2. In the assessment of mental retardation, discuss the different functions of norm-referenced and criterion-referenced instruments.

3. Describe the Leiter International Performance Scale and discuss its psychometric characteristics and adequacy.

4. List the major provisions of Public Law 94-142.

TEST ITEM FILE

Topic 7A: Testing Special Populations

1. The Public Law known as the "Bill of Rights" for disabled persons was passed in
    a. 1943
    b. 1953
    c. 1963
    *d. 1973

2. Public Law 94-142 is the
    *a. Education for All Handicapped Children Act
    b. Anti-Discrimination Act for Handicapped Persons
    c. Education to Prevent Poverty Act
    d. none of the above

3. The Education for All Handicapped Children Act was designed to
    a. insure that special education services are available to children who need them
    b. guarantee that decisions about services to handicapped students are fair and appropriate
    c. provide federal funds to help the states educate handicapped students
    *d. all of the above

4. The Education for All Handicapped Children Act contains the following provision(s):
    a. tests are to be selected and administered in such a way as to be racially and culturally nondiscriminatory
    b. tests used with students must include those designed to provide information about specific educational needs
    c. evaluations are to be made by a multidisciplinary team that includes at least one teacher
    *d. all of the above

5. Regarding student placement, the Education for All Handicapped Children Act specifies that
    a. handicapped children should be placed in the least restrictive environment
    b. separate schooling is allowed if the nature or the severity of the handicap is such that instructional goals cannot be achieved in the regular classroom
    *c. both a and b
    d. neither a nor b

6. Amendments to the Education for All Handicapped Children Act
    a. require states to provide a free appropriate public education to handicapped children ages three through five
    b. provide financial grants to states that offer interdisciplinary educational services to handicapped infants, toddlers, and their families
    *c. both a and b
    d. neither a nor b

7. Instructions for the Leiter International Performance Scale
    a. are standardized through the use of a tape recorded, step-by-step message
    b. require the examiner to demonstrate the first several test items
    *c. are minimal or nonexistent since the nature of the test is obvious
    d. none of the above

8. The Leiter International Performance Scale has two kinds of items, conceptual and
    a. analytical
    b. problem-solving
    c. verbal
    *d. perceptual

9. Correlations between the Leiter International Performance Scale and the Stanford-Binet are in the
    a. .30s   c. 50s
    b. .40s   *d. 60s

10. The Leiter International Performance Scale has the following problem(s):
    a. the norms are weak and outdated
    b. the reliability of the test is open to question
    *c. both a and b
    d. neither a nor b

11. The Goodenough-Harris Drawing Test is a(n)
    a. projective measure of personality
    b. measure of intellectual giftedness
    *c. index of intellectual maturity
    d. none of the above

12. The instructions for the Goodenough-Harris Drawing Test convey that the examinee should draw
    *a. a picture of a man
    b. anything of interest to the examinee
    c. a family consisting of husband, wife, son, and daughter
    d. a house, tree, and person

13. The standardization sample for the Goodenough-Harris Drawing Test consisted of about _____ persons.
    a. 30
    b. 300
    *c. 3,000
    d. 30,000

14. Commonly, split-half reliabilities of the Goodenough-Harris Drawing Test are about
    a. .30
    b. .50
    c. .70
    *d. .90

15. Interscorer reliability of the Goodenough-Harris Drawing Test is typically
    a. .30   c. .70
    b. .50   *d. .90

16. Correlations between the Goodenough-Harris Drawing Test and the WPPSI are typically in the range of
    a. .10 to .20
    b. .30 to .40
    c. .50 to .60
    *d. .70 to .80

17. The Goodenough-Harris Drawing Test is considered especially appropriate for
   a. minority children
   b. hearing-impaired children
   c. visually-impaired children
   *d. all of the above

18. The Hiskey-Nebraska Test of Learning Aptitude was specially designed for _____ children.
   *a. hearing-impaired
   b. visually-impaired
   c. cognitively impaired
   d. minority

19. Using the Hiskey-Nebraska for purposes of classification increases the risk of
   a. labeling children as gifted when they are only bright
   b. classifying children as retarded when they are merely borderline
   *c. both a and b
   d. neither a nor b

20. Hiskey-Nebraska scores correlate about _____ with WISC-R Performance IQ.
   a. .25   c. 65
   b. .45   *d. 85

21. Items on the Test of Nonverbal Intelligence-2 consist of
   a. simple matching
   b. analogies
   c. classification
   *d. all of the above

22. Items were selected for the Test of Nonverbal Intelligence-2 on the basis of
   a. item-total correlations
   b. difficulty level
   c. acceptability to users
   *d. all of the above

23. The format of the items in the Test of Nonverbal Intelligence-2 is very similar to
    a. Leiter International Performance Scale
    b. Shipley Institute of Living Scale
  *c. Raven's Progressive Matrices
    d. none of the above

24. The age range for the Test of Nonverbal Intelligence-2 is
    a. 5 through 12   c. 5 through 65
    b. 5 through 15   *d. 5 through 85

25. Validity studies support the view(s) that the Test of Nonverbal Intelligence-2 is
  *a. a good measure of general intelligence
    b. mainly a measure of nonverbal intelligence
    c. both a and b
    d. neither a nor b

26. Persons with cerebral palsy may show
    a. motor deficits
    b. tendency to fatigue
    c. problems with purposive movements
  *d. all of the above

27. The best known and most widely used of the nonreading, motor-reduced tests is the
    a. Test of Nonverbal Intelligence-2
    b. Goodenough-Harris Drawing Test
  *c. Peabody Picture Vocabulary Test-Revised
    d. Columbia Mental Maturity Scale

28. The format for the Peabody Picture Vocabulary Test-Revised is:
  *a. from four line drawings, the examinee points to the single choice which best illustrates a spoken word
    b. from a single line drawing, the examinee identifies the typed word which is best exemplified by the drawing
    c. the examinee draws a picture to illustrate each word in a list of words of increasing difficulty
    d. none of the above

29. The Peabody Picture Vocabulary Test-Revised has questionable applicability to persons over the age of
    a. 20
    *b. 40
    c. 60
    d. 80

30. Validity studies support the use of the Peabody Picture Vocabulary Test-Revised as a
    *a. narrow measure of vocabulary
    b. general measure of intelligence
    c. specific measure of pictorial intelligence
    d. all of the above

31. One caution in using the Peabody Picture Vocabulary Test-Revised is that the standard scores
    a. have an atypical standard deviation of 10
    *b. may be lower than Wechsler IQs for minorities
    c. are based upon a very small standardization sample
    d. all of the above

32. The Columbia Mental Maturity Scale was originally devised for
    a. young children with hearing impairments
    *b. young children with cerebral palsy
    c. older adults with poor reading skills
    d. older adults with visual impairments

33. Test-retest reliability coefficients for the Columbia Mental Maturity Scale are in the high
    a. .20s
    b. .40s
    c. .60s
    *d. .80s

34. A young child who merely guesses on the Columbia Mental Maturity Scale will, on average, obtain a score of about
    a. 40   *c. 80
    b. 60   d. 100

35. What is the content of the Perkins-Binet?
    a. retains verbal items only from the Stanford-Binet
    *b. retains verbal items and includes adapted tactual items
    c. retains performance items only
    d. none of the above

36. Most of the items from the Blind Learning Aptitude Test were adapted from
    a. Raven's Progressive Matrices
    b. Culture Free Intelligence Test
    c. Stanford-Binet
    *d. both a and b

37. Mental retardation is defined as
    a. significantly subaverage general intellectual functioning
    b. impairments in adaptive behavior
    c. difficulties arise before age 18
    *d. all of the above

38. An IQ in the mentally retarded range is at least ____ standard deviation below average.
    a. one
    *b. two
    c. three
    d. four

39. How many levels of mental retardation are formally recognized by diagnostic manuals?
    a. one
    b. two
    c. three
    *d. four

40. The definition of adaptive behavior emphasizes
    a. personal independence
    b. social responsibility
    *c. both a and b
    d. neither a nor b

41. The first standardized instrument for assessing adaptive behavior was the
   *a. Vineland Social Maturity Scale
   b. Columbia Mental Maturity Scale
   c. Scales of Independent Behavior
   d. Vineland Adaptive Behavior Scales

42. For training and rehabilitation purposes, examiners might wish to use a(n) _____ measure of adaptive behavior.
   a. norm-referenced
   *b. criterion-referenced
   c. intelligence-based
   d. none of the above

43. The Scales of Independent Behavior assesses
   a. motor skills
   b. social and communication skills
   c. personal living skills
   *d. all of the above

44. The Scales of Independent Behavior are co-normed with the
   a. Stanford-Binet: Fourth Edition
   b. Wechsler Adult Intelligence Scale-Revised
   c. Peabody Picture Vocabulary Test-Revised
   *d. Woodcock-Johnson Psychoeducational Battery

45. For mentally handicapped subjects, overall score on the Scales of Independent Behavior correlates about ____ with IQ.
   a. .2
   b. .4
   c. .6
   *d. .8

46. The items on the Independent Living Behavior Checklist specify a
   a. condition
   b. behavior
   c. standard
   *d. all of the above

47. The Independent Living Behavior Checklist is
    *a. norm-referenced
    b. criterion-referenced
    c. both a and b
    d. neither a nor b

48. Which of the following is NOT an adaptive behavior scale or checklist?
    a. Balthazar Scales of Adaptive Behavior
    b. Camelot Behavioral Checklist
    c. T.M.R. School Competency Scales
    *d. Seguin-Goddard Behavior Scales

Topic 7B

Test Bias and Other Controversies

The Question of Test Bias

    The Test Bias Controversy
    Criteria of Test Bias and Test Fairness
    The Technical Meaning of Test Bias: A Definition
    Bias in Content Validity
    Bias in Predictive or Criterion-Related Validity
    Bias in Construct Validity
    Reprise on Test Bias

Social Values and Test Fairness
    Unqualified Individualism
    Quotas
    Qualified Individualism
    Reprise on Test Fairness

Genetic and Environmental Determinants of Intelligence

    Genetic Contributions to Intelligence
    Environmental Effects: Impoverishment and Enrichment
    Teratogenic Effects on Intelligence and Development
    Effects of Environmental Toxins on Intelligence

Origins of African-American and White IQ Differences

    African American and White IQ Differences
    The Genetic Hypothesis for Race Differences
    Tenability of the Genetic Hypothesis

Age Changes in Intelligence

    Early Cross-sectional Research
    Sequential Studies of Intelligence
    Postformal Operations in Adulthood and Old Age

Generational Changes in Intelligence Test Scores

Summary

Key Terms and Concepts

Classroom Discussion Questions

1. The general topic of test bias is almost guaranteed to generate intense classroom discussion. Do students believe that existing tests (especially ability tests) are culturally biased? What evidence can they cite to support their opinions?

2. The text discusses three philosophies of test fairness in selection: unqualified individualism, quotas, and qualified individualism. Which position do students support? Why?

3. What does it mean to assert, as does the text, that intelligence has a substantial genetic component? Do students agree with this assertion? An important point to make in the context of this discussion is that objective methods exist for determining the extent of genetic influence (e.g., heritability index with twins; adoption studies).

4. What is the logic of the adoption method discussed in the text? Do students understand the Honzik study and similar approaches to the study of intelligence?

5. Is the study of race differences in intelligence a legitimate topic for scientists? Some persons assert that certain topics are so fraught with potential for racist consequences that scientific investigation should be postponed. How do students feel about racial comparisons on psychological tests?

6. A topic worthy of discussion is the relationship between age and intelligence. Ask students to offer their opinions on the nature of age changes in intelligence. What is the basis for their opinions?

7. What are some possible explanations for the fact that African-Americans score lower on IQ tests than whites?

Extramural Assignments

1. Ask students to read and summarize one or more of McGurk's (1953ab, 1967, 1975) articles on test bias.

2. Arthur Jensen's position on black-white IQ differences is so frequently misunderstood that is useful to ask students to read his original paper: Jensen, A. R. (1969). How much can we boost IQ and scholastic achievement? Harvard Educational Review, 39, 1-123. Oral or written reports might be required.

3. The role of environmental toxins in producing behavioral and intellectual deficits is now a topic of widespread study. Ask students to find recent articles and summarize the findings for presentation to the class. Lead poisoning and fetal alcohol syndrome are two of the most widely studied topics in this area.

Classroom Demonstrations

1. Use a child's test such as the WISC-R or WISC-III to initiate a discussion of test bias. Which items "seem" biased to students? What kinds of studies would be needed to corroborate these suspicions of test bias? What is test bias, anyway?

2. Organize a debate on the question of selection philosophies in test fairness. Have students argue the merits of quotas versus individualism, etc.

3. Invite a gerontologist or other expert in aging to class to discuss intellectual changes and assessment in the elderly. Be sure to emphasize the potentially confounding role of post-formal thought in old age, that is, tests designed for young persons may not be fair to post-formal thinkers.

Essay Questions

1. Define test bias. How does the concept of test bias differ from the concept of test fairness?

2. What kinds of evidence can be cited to show that a test is biased?

3. Discuss the characteristics of post-formal thought.

4. Apparently, from 1932 to 1981 the average IQ of the American population rose 14 points. What are some possible explanations for this apparent gain?

5. Describe the nature of intellectual changes from young adulthood to old age.

6. What kinds of evidence support the assertion that intelligence has a significant genetic component?

TEST ITEM FILE

Topic 7B: Test Bias and Other Controversies

1. Which concept incorporates and reflects social values?
    a. test bias
    *b. test fairness
    c. both a and b
    d. neither a nor b

2. When socioeconomic disparities are taken into account, the average African-American White IQ difference is on the order of _____ points.
    a. 0 to 3
    *b. 7 to 10
    c. 15 to 18
    d. 21 to 24

3. Which of the following is a sufficient basis for indicating test bias?
   a. large differences in scores between defined subpopulations
   b. the appearance of preference for one group in item content
   c. absence of a defined subpopulation in the standardization
   *d. none of the above

4. A significant sex difference has been shown in the area of
   a. general problem solving
   b. concept formation
   *c. spatial thinking
   d. design copying

5. The textbook takes the general position that test bias is synonymous with
   a. test fairness
   b. unintended outcomes of test usage
   c. differences between defined subpopulations
   *d. differential validity

6. An item or subscale of a test is considered to have bias in
   _____ when it is demonstrated to be relatively more
   difficult for members of one group than another when the general
   ability level of the groups being compared is held constant and no
   reasonable theoretical rationale exists to explain group differences on
   the item (or subscale) in question.
   *a. content validity
   b. criterion-related validity
   c. construct validity
   d. face validity

7. According to McGurk's analysis, items nominated by experts as
   "most cultural" are _____ for blacks compared to whites.
   *a. relatively less difficult
   b. relatively more difficult
   c. about equal in difficulty
   d. none of the above

8. A test is considered to have bias in _____ when the inference drawn from the test score is not made with the smallest feasible random error or if there is constant error in an inference or prediction as a function of membership in a particular group.
   a. content validity
   *b. criterion-related validity
   c. construct validity
   d. face validity

9. According to the criterion of homogeneous regression, a test is unbiased if
   *a. the results for all relevant subpopulations cluster equally well around a single regression line
   b. each subpopulation produces a regression line with similar slope
   c. there is no single regression line that works equally well for relevant subpopulations
   d. none of the above

10. In the equation $Y = bX + a$, the slope of the regression line is
   a. Y
   b. a
   c. X
   *d. b

11. In the equation $Y = bX + a$, the predicted grade point average would be
   *a. Y
   b. a
   c. X
   d. b

12. In the equation $Y = bX + a$, the score on the predictor test would be
   a. Y
   b. a
   *c. X
   d. b

13. With the Scholastic Aptitude Test, a consistent finding with respect to African-American and white examinees is that
   *a. separate, parallel regression lines are needed
   b. a single homogeneous regression line works best
   c. separate, nonparallel regression lines are needed
   d. none of the above

14. With respect to African-American and white examinees, it appears that the Scholastic Aptitude Test
   *a. overpredicts the performance of African-American examinees
   b. underpredicts the performance of African-American examinees
   c. overpredicts the performance of white examinees
   d. both b and c

15. A test is said to show bias in _____ construct validity when it measures different hypothetical traits (psychological constructs) for one group than another or measures the same trait but with differing degrees of accuracy.
   a. content validity
   b. criterion-related validity
   *c. construct validity
   d. face validity

16. In general, for prominent ability and aptitude tests, the rank order of item difficulties is _____ for relevant subpopulations.
   a. greatly dissimilar
   b. moderately dissimilar
   *c. virtually identical
   d. unknown

17. According to the philosophy of _____, without exception, the best qualified candidates should be selected for employment, admission, or other privilege.
   a. qualified individualism
   b. quotas
   *c. unqualified individualism
   d. selective fitness

18. One potentially troubling implication of unqualified individualism as a philosophy of test usage is that
    a. minorities never get a chance to be hired
    b. the majority group usually defines the test
    *c. race or sex may prove to be valid predictors
    d. none of the above

19. Since bureaucracies and educational institutions exist at the will of the people, it can be argued that these institutions are ethically bound to act in a manner that is "politically appropriate" to their location. This is the philosophy of
    a. qualified individualism
    *b. quotas
    c. unqualified individualism
    d. selective fitness

20. According to the philosophy of _____, it is ethically inappropriate to use race or sex in employment decisions.
    a. qualified individualism
    b. quotas
    *c. unqualified individualism
    d. selective fitness

21. A heritability index can vary between
    a. -1.0 and +1.0
    *b. 0.0 and +1.0
    c. -100 to +100
    d. 0 to 100

22. Heritability has which characteristic(s)?
    a. it is a population statistic
    b. it is not constant for a specific trait
    c. it depends upon the point in time
    *d. all of the above

23. For IQ, most studies report heritability estimates right around
    *a. .50   c. 30
    b. .80   d. 60

24. When adopted children are repeatedly tested with an instrument
such as the Stanford-Binet, their intelligence correlates
*a. more closely with that of their biological parents
b. more closely with that of their adoptive parents
c. about equally well with biological and adoptive parents
d. with neither biological nor adoptive parents

25. According to Jensen's study of cumulative deficit, African-
American children in an impoverished environment lose about ____ IQ
point(s) a year between the ages of 5 and 16.
a. 1/2
*b. 1
c. 2
d. 3

26. According to Scarr and Weinberg's research, African-American
children adopted into middle-class white families early in life, before
age one, showed an average IQ of
a. 90
b. 100
*c. 110
d. 120

27. In general, studies show that intervention and enrichment
_____ in children at risk for school failure and mental
retardation.
*a. can boost IQ
b. have no effect on IQ
c. have an unpredictable effect on IQ
d. causes a mild IQ decline

28. Fetal alcohol syndrome has the following characteristic(s):
a. unusual facial appearance
b. low IQ
c. poor muscle tone
*d. all of the above

29. Which problem is more severe, fetal alcohol syndrome or fetal alcohol effect?
  *a. fetal alcohol syndrome
  b. fetal alcohol effect
  c. no difference--the terms are synonymous
  d. these competing diagnostic terms cannot be compared

30. High doses of lead are linked to
  a. cerebral palsy
  b. seizure disorders
  c. mental retardation
  *d. all of the above

31. In some studies, asymptomatic lead exposure is associated with an average decrement of about ___ points in IQ.
  *a. 4
  b. 9
  c. 14
  d. 24

32. On the average, African-Americans score about ___ points lower than white Americans on standardized IQ tests.
  a. 5
  b. 10
  *c. 15
  d. 20

33. When demographic variables such as socioeconomic status are taken into account, the size of the mean African-American white IQ difference
  a. remains unchanged
  b. increases slightly
  *c. decreases by 1/3 to 1/2
  d. decreases to zero

34. The genetic hypothesis of African-American white IQ differences has the following problem(s):
    a. heritability within groups cannot be used to infer heritability between groups
    b. the degree of African ancestry does not help predict average IQs within black subgroups
    *c. both a and b
    d. neither a nor b

35. According to Lynn, the mean IQ for Japanese is estimated to be
    a. 97   *c. 107
    b. 102   d. 112

36. Regarding the fate of intelligence with advancing age, early cross-sectional research was
    *a. pessimistic
    b. neutral
    c. mildly optimistic
    d. very optimistic

37. Wechsler believed that raw intelligence _____ with advancing age.
    *a. declined
    b. remained stable
    c. increased slightly
    d. increased significantly

38. Longitudinal studies suffer from the following pitfall(s):
    a. selective attrition
    b. practice effects
    c. regression to the mean
    *d. all of the above

39. A cross-sequential design
    *a. combines cross-sectional and longitudinal methods
    b. is the same thing as a longitudinal design
    c. is preferred because it is less expensive
    d. all of the above

40. Regarding age changes in intelligence, results from longitudinal studies are generally _____ results from cross-sectional studies.
   *a. more optimistic than
   b. on a par with
   c. more pessimistic than
   d. none of the above

41. According to Schaie, the vast majority of us show no meaningful decline in the skills measured by the Primary Mental Abilities Test until we are well into our
   a. fifties
   b. sixties
   *c. seventies
   d. eighties

42. Piaget believed that adult development beyond formal thought was
   *a. impossible
   b. possible but not probable
   c. possible and likely
   d. commonplace

43. Formal operational thought emphasizes
   *a. problem solving
   b. problem finding
   c. both a and b
   d. neither a nor b

44. Postformal thinking has the following general characteristic(s):
   a. recognition that knowledge is relative and temporary
   b. acceptance of contradiction as a basic aspect of reality
   c. ability to synthesize contradictory thoughts, emotions, and experiences
   *d. all of the above

45. Apparently, what happened to the IQ of the American population between 1930 and 1980?
   a. there was no change
   b. average IQ declined by 3-5 points
   c. average IQ increased by 3-5 points
   *d. average IQ increased by 13-15 points

46. Flynn's interpretation of generational IQ changes is that
   *a. we should stop saying that IQ tests measure intelligence
   b. educational innovations have actually boosted intelligence
   c. nutritional changes are the main explanation
   d. none of the above

Topic 8A

Aptitude Tests and Factor Analysis

A Primer of Factor Analysis

    The Correlation Matrix
    The Factor Matrix and Factor Loadings
    Geometric Representation of Factor Loadings
    The Rotated Factor Matrix
    The Interpretation of Factors
    Issues in Factor Analysis

Multiple Aptitude Test Batteries

    The Differential Aptitude Test (DAT)
    The General Aptitude Test Battery (GATB)
    The Armed Services Vocational Aptitude Battery (ASVAB)

Predicting College Performance

    The Scholastic Assessment Test (SAT)
    The American College Test (ACT)

Summary

Key Terms and Concepts

Classroom Discussion Questions

1. Most college students have taken the SAT or the ACT. Solicit their opinions of these tests. How well did the results predict college performance in individual cases?

2. SAT scores declined precipitously from the 1960s to the mid 1980s. Have students propose possible explanations for this decline.

Extramural Assignments

1. Request that students find an example of factor analysis in a psychology journal. Also ask them to bring the results of the factor analysis (input, factor matrix, interpretation, etc.) to class for discussion.

Classroom Demonstrations

1. Invite a university admissions official to class to discuss the role of scholastic aptitude tests in college admissions.

2. Prepare overhead transparencies which illustrate the process of factor analysis. The three-factor solution to the Wechsler Scales is useful because students can readily identify the relationship between emergent factors and subtests. Silverstein (1977, 1982ab) provides many examples.

Essay Questions

1. How are factors named in factor analysis? Give a hypothetical but realistic example of how a factor might be named.

2. Describe the Armed Services Vocational Aptitude Battery and discuss its strengths and weaknesses.

TEST ITEM FILE

Topic 8A: Aptitude Tests and Factor Analysis

1. The purpose of factor analysis is to:
   *a. help produce a parsimonious description of large, complex data sets
   b. discover the correlations that exist between tests or variables
   c. produce a larger number of factors from a smaller number of tests or variables
   d. none of the above

2. The beginning point for every factor analysis is the
   a. factor matrix
   *b. correlation matrix
   c. table of factor loadings
   d. none of the above

3. The factor matrix consists of a table of correlations called
   a. matrix loadings
   b. correlation vectors
   c. matrix vectors
   *d. factor loadings

4. Statistically speaking, a factor is
   a. the intercorrelation between variables
   b. the sum total of the matrix loadings
   *c. a weighted linear sum of the variables
   d. none of the above

5. Statistically speaking, factor loadings are
   *a. correlation coefficients between variables and factors
   b. the intercorrelation between variables
   c. the sum total of the matrix loadings
   d. a weighted linear sum of the variables

6. In producing the final rotated factor matrix, researchers often rely upon
    a. the criterion of positive manifold
    b. the criterion of simple structure
    *c. both a and b
    d. neither a nor b

7. The naming of factors depends upon
    a. statistical analysis
    *b. reasoned judgment
    c. the name of the test with the highest loading
    d. inferring what non-loading tests share in common

8. What are marker tests?
    *a. tests from a larger battery that best depict the major factors
    b. tests which have near zero loadings on the major factors
    c. both a and b
    d. neither a nor b

9. A particular kind of factor can emerge from factor analysis
    a. regardless of the kinds of tests used, so long as the number of subjects is very large
    *b. only if the tests and measures contain that factor in the first place
    c. only if the proper kind of factor analysis is selected
    d. none of the above

10. In factor analysis, Comrey rates a sample size of 500 as
    a. fair
    b. good
    *c. very good
    d. excellent

11. In factor analysis, it is desirable to have a minimum of ___ subjects for each test or variable.
    a. 1
    *b. 5
    c. 10
    d. 100

12. With orthogonal axes the factors are
    a. at right angles to one another
    b. uncorrelated
    *c. both a and b
    d. neither a nor b

13. With oblique axes the factors are
    a. at right angles to one another
    b. uncorrelated
    *c. correlated among themselves
    d. none of the above

14. With _____ rotations it is also possible to factor analyze the factors themselves.
    a. orthogonal
    *b. oblique
    c. both a and b
    d. neither a nor b

15. When the factors are factor analyzed, the outcome consists of
    *a. second-order factors
    b. oblique factors
    c. orthogonal factors
    d. none of the above

16. The Primary Mental Abilities Test was developed by
    a. Spearman
    *b. Thurstone
    c. Wechsler
    d. Strong

17. The Differential Aptitude Test consists of ____ independent tests.
    a. 2
    b. 4
    c. 6
    *d. 8

18. The norms for the Differential Aptitude Test are based upon _____ individuals.
    a. 60
    b. 600
    c. 6,000
    *d. 60,000

19. The split-half reliability of the Differential Aptitude Test is generally in the
    a. .60s
    b. .70s
    c. .80s
    *d. .90s

20. The scholastic aptitude index on the Differential Aptitude Test consists of
    a. abstract reasoning and language usage
    b. verbal reasoning and abstract reasoning
    *c. verbal reasoning and numerical aptitude
    d. language usage and numerical aptitude

21. The General Aptitude Test Battery is composed of
    *a. eight paper-and-pencil tests and four apparatus measures
    b. eight paper-and-pencil tests and two apparatus measures
    c. eight paper-and-pencil tests
    d. six paper-and-pencil tests

22. The nine factor scores on the General Aptitude Test Battery are expressed as standard scores with a mean of _____ and an SD of _____.
    a. 50, 10   c. 100, 10
    b. 50, 20   *d. 100, 20

23. On the General Aptitude Test Battery, the nine specific factor scores combine nicely into three general factors:
    *a. Cognitive, Perceptual, and Psychomotor
    b. Cognitive, Numerical, and Psychomotor
    c. Cognitive, Perceptual, and Spatial
    d. Cognitive, Numerical, and Spatial

24. The _____ is probably the most widely used paper-and-pencil test in existence.
    a. General Aptitude Test Battery
    b. Differential Aptitude Test
    *c. Armed Services Vocational Aptitude Battery
    d. Primary Mental Abilities Test

25. The ASVAB manual reports a median validity coefficient of ___ with measures of training performance.
    a. .20
    b. .40
   *c. .60
    d. .80

26. A particular weakness of the ASVAB is that
    a. standardization data are inadequate
    b. the reliability of the subtests is marginal
   *c. a subtest may occur in more than one composite
    d. the validity of the test is unproven

27. The average intercorrelation among the composite scores of the ASVAB is about
    a. .30
    b. .50
    c. .70
   *d. .90

28. The oldest of the college admission tests is the
   *a. Scholastic Assessment Test
    b. American College Testing Program
    c. Graduate Record Examination
    d. Law School Admission Test

29. The subtests of the Scholastic Assessment Test consist of
    a. Verbal and Spatial
    b. Word Usage and Spatial
   *c. Verbal and Mathematics
    d. Word Usage and Mathematics

30. In general, scores on an SAT subtest can range from
    a. 0 to 100
    b. 0 to 1000
    c. 50 to 150
   *d. 200 to 800

31. The standard deviation of SAT subtest scores is
    a. 10
    b. 15
    c. 50
  *d. 100

32. In any given year, the mean of SAT subtest scores will be
    a. 50
    b. 100
    c. 500
  *d. unknown

33. From 1963 into the middle 1980s, SAT scores
    a. remained stable
    b. increased slightly
    c. declined and then increased
  *d. declined significantly

34. Long-term shifts in SAT scores have been related to
  *a. changes in average family size
    b. nutritional status of the examinees
    c. relaxation of educational standards
    d. all of the above

35. The standard error of measurement of SAT subtests is
  *a. 35
    b. 70
    c. 100
    d. none of the above

36. On average, combined SAT scores correlate ____ with college freshman GPA.
    a. .2
  *b. .4
    c. .6
    d. .8

37. The effect of coaching on SAT subtest scores is to increase scores about ___ points.
  a. 0
  *b. 15
  c. 50
  d. 100

38. Students who retake the SATs within five to eight months score ___ points higher, on average.
  a. 2
  *b. 12
  c. 25
  d. 50

39. English Usage, Mathematics Usage, Social Studies Reading, and Natural Sciences Reading are the four subtests of the _____.
  a. SAT
  b. GRE
  *c. ACT
  d. none of the above

40. On the ACT, the predictive validity coefficients are
  *a. virtually identical for advantaged and disadvantaged students
  b. better for white students than for African-American students
  c. better for students of high social class than low social class
  d. better for bright students than less bright students

41. Critics of the ACT program have pointed to the heavy emphasis upon
  a. mathematics
  b. factual knowledge
  c. test wiseness
  *d. reading comprehension

Topic 8B

Achievement Tests and Learning Disability Assessment

Essential Concepts in Achievement Testing

Group and Individual Achievement Tests
Norm-referenced and Criterion-referenced Tests
Ability, Aptitude, and Achievement Tests
The Functions of Achievement Testing

Educational Achievement Tests

Iowa Tests of Basic Skills
Metropolitan Achievement Test
The Iowa Tests of Educational Development
The Tests of Achievement and Proficiency
Tests of General Educational Development (GED)
Additional Group Standardized Achievement Tests

Individual Achievement Tests

Merits of Individual Achievement Tests
Overview of Individual Achievement Tests
Kaufman Test of Educational Achievement (K-TEA)

Assessment of Learning Disabilities

The Definition of Learning Disabilities
Essential Features of Learning Disabilities
Test Batteries in the Assessment of Learning Disabilities

Assessment of Attention-deficit/Hyperactivity Disorder

Summary

Key Terms and Concepts

Classroom Discussion Questions

1. Ask students to discuss the differences between aptitude, ability, and achievement tests. What is their understanding of these different instruments? How well do their conceptions mirror the distinctions given in the textbook?

2. Ask students to discuss their understanding of learning disability. How well do their conceptions mirror the viewpoints listed in the textbook?

3. Ask if any students previously diagnosed as learning disabled would be willing to share their perceptions with the class. Often, such students are open to discussing their frustrations. Further, they can shed light on the role of psychological testing in the assessment of these disorders.

4. What is an attention deficit disorder? Solicit opinions from students on the characteristics of the so-called hyperactive child. The instructor might find it useful to list points on the blackboard as the discussion proceeds. Then, compare the students' conceptions with the formal criteria listed in topic 8B.

Extramural Assignments

1. A topic of great interest to many students is the role of drug therapy in the treatment of hyperactive children. Request that students find journal articles that discuss the effects of Ritalin (methylphenidate) on hyperactive or attention-disordered children. In particular, what kinds of psychological tests or rating scales were used to determine the drug effects?

2. Another topic of interest to most students is the role of psychological testing in the diagnosis of learning disabilities. Ask students to find journal articles that use psychological tests in the assessment of learning disabilities. What tests were used? Which criteria were consulted to determine the existence of learning disabilities?

3. An ambitious project would be for students to design an anonymous questionnaire on the presence of learning disabilities in a sample of college students. When guaranteed anonymity, what percentage of college students will admit that they have been formally diagnosed as learning disabled? What kinds of tests do they recall taking in order to receive the diagnosis?

Classroom Demonstrations

1. Ask a school psychologists to come in to class and discuss the role of achievement tests in the assessment of learning disabilities. Also, the consultant can be asked about local criteria, the role of social politics in the designation of who is LD, etc.

2. Items from children's achievement tests can be demonstrated to the class as a means of generating discussion. With permission and appropriate informed consent, a psychologist can also administer an achievement test to a child.

3. Rating scales for hyperactivity (e.g., the ACTeRS, discussed in text) can be demonstrated to the class. An interesting exercise would be for students to rate (from memory) a child they know well and discuss the results with the class.

Essay Questions

1. Discuss the GED and its comparability to receiving a high school diploma by attending school.

2. Discuss the definition of learning disabilities.

3. Describe a useful test battery for the assessment of possible learning disability in a fifteen year old boy.

4. Give the name of one useful group test of educational achievement and discuss its general characteristics.

TEST ITEM FILE

Topic 8B: Achievement Tests and Learning Disability Assessment

1. The purpose of achievement tests is to measure
   *a. current skill level in a well-defined domain
   b. potential achievement level in a well-defined domain
   c. general ability as it pertains to a specific skill
   d. all of the above

2. Individual achievement tests play an essential role in the
   a. screening of mentally retarded persons
   b. measurement of school-related aptitude
   *c. diagnosis of a learning disability
   d. all of the above

3. A reasonable estimate is that about ___ percent of all elementary and secondary students can be classified as learning disabled.
   *a. 5   c. 15
   b. 10   d. 20

4. Tests used to predict future performance are known as _____ tests.
   *a. aptitude
   b. achievement
   c. both a and b
   d. neither a nor b

5. Achievement tests can be used to
   a. appraise the success of educational programs by measuring the subsequent skill attainment of students
   b. group students according to similar skill level in specific academic domains
   c. identify the level of instruction that is appropriate for individual students
   *d. all of the above

6. The essential feature of tests that are concurrently normed is:
   *a. they share the same standardization sample
   b. they were normed at the same time
   c. they have the same average and standard deviation
   d. they measure the same underlying constructs

7. The purpose of the Iowa Tests of Basic Skills is to
   a. detect weaknesses in school system curricula
   b. screen elementary school children for potential learning disabilities
   c. identify children who are underachieving
   *d. provide information which can be used to improve instruction

8. Typically, the correlation between scores on the Iowa Tests of Basic Skills and high school grades is about
   a. .2   *c. .6
   b. .4   d. .8

9. Regarding the Metropolitan Achievement Test, reviewers have noted the need for additional evidence of
   a. reliability
   b. content validity
   *c. criterion-related validity
   d. all of the above

10. Which test is designed to measure the fundamental goals or generalized skills of education that are independent of the curriculum?
    a. Metropolitan Achievement Test, Sixth Edition
    b. Iowa Tests of Basic Skills
    *c. Iowa Tests of Educational Development
    d. Tests of Achievement and Proficiency

11. In general, the GED (Tests of General Educational Development) is considered _____ a regular high school diploma.
    a. much easier than
    b. slightly easier than
    *c. more difficult than
    d. about on a par with

12. Subtests from the Kaufman Test of Educational Achievement assess all of the following EXCEPT
    a. reading comprehension
    b. mathemathics applications
    c. spelling
    *d. writing proficiency

13. Results on the Kaufman Test of Educational Achievement can be expressed as
    a. standard scores
    b. qualitative errors
    *c. both a and b
    d. neither a nor b

14. Perhaps the most widely used definition of learning disabilities is
    *a. the one mandated by Public Law 94-142
    b. the rehabilitation agency viewpoint
    c. the deficit model proposed by Cruickshank
    d. none of the above

15. In reference to learning disabilities, a severe discrepancy refers to a difference of at least _____ standard deviation(s).
    *a. one   c. three
    b. two   d. four

16. If an apparent learning difficult is primarily caused by _____, then a learning disability cannot be diagnosed.
    a. visual problems
    b. mental retardation
    c. economic disadvantage
    *d. all of the above

17. Cruickshank's view is that learning disabilities are _____ neurological in origin.
    a. never
    b. rarely
    c. usually
    *d. always

18. Most definitions of learning disabilities emphasize
    a. a discrepancy between ability and achievement
    b. the exclusion of certain causes
    c. onset in childhood
    *d. all of the above

19. The Personality Inventory for Children is
    a. a true-false inventory
    b. filled out by the parents
    c. empirically keyed
    *d. all of the above

20. The various Conners' scales for hyperactivity and behavior disorders are
    *a. four point rating scales
    b. true false inventories
    c. bipolar rarting scales
    d. none of the above

21. In factor analyses of the Conners' scales, the first and by far the most prominent factor is
    a. general maladjustment
    *b. hyperactivity
    c. conduct disorder
    d. anxiety

22. Which of the below is NOT a subtype of ADHD?
    a. Inattentive
    b. Hyperactive-Impulsive
    c. Aggressive
    d. Combined

23. Which of the below is a diagnostic symptom of ADHD?
    a. loses things
    b. talks excessively
    c. fidgets and/or squirms
    d. all of the above

Topic 9A

A Primer of Neuropsychology

Anatomy of the Brain

Case Exhibit 9.1: Brain Dysfunction and Test Results

Functional Organization of the Brain

Hindbrain
Midbrain
Diencephalon
Limbic Lobe
Basal Ganglia
Corpus Callosum
Cerebral Cortex

Functions of the Frontal, Parietal, Temporal, and Occipital Lobes

Occipital Lobes
Parietal Lobes
Temporal Lobes
Frontal Lobes

Lateralization of Function Within the Cerebral Hemispheres

Language Functions of the Left Hemisphere

Specialized Functions of the Right Cerebral Hemisphere

Clinical Tests and Brain-Imaging Techniques

Applications of Neuropsychological Test Findings

Summary

Key Terms and Concepts

Classroom Discussion Questions

1. The number of different approaches to learning about brain function might surprise students. Have students discuss how neuroscientists have learned about brain function.

2. As part of a general review of brain structures and their functions, the instructor might ask students to discuss the kinds of tests that might be used to assess specific brain functions. For example, it is known that the reticular activating system governs the general level of arousal. What kind of test might be used to assess these functions?

3. What are the characteristics and functions of different brain imaging techniques? The instructor can list the methods and ask students to discuss what they know about each. Perhaps some students have had direct or indirect experience with one or techniques, e.g., perhaps a relative had to take a CT scan after a head injury.

4. What are the differential functions of the left and right cerebral hemispheres? The instructor can make a list on the blackboard as the discussion proceeds.

Extramural Assignments

1. Have students solicit information from hospitals and clinics as to the kinds of brain imaging techniques used. Most such settings will have free informational brochures which can be valuable sources of information. Perhaps small groups of students could arrange a visit to the facilities to observe the machines in operation.

2. Assign students the task of summarizing brain structures and functions in a single, comprehensive diagram.

3. A difficult assignment would be for students to find one or more articles, from neurology or neuropsychology journals, that discuss the role of tests in determining brain functions. For example, what are the

consequences of certain neurosurgical procedures upon brain functions? What tests were used to determine those consequences?

Classroom Demonstrations

1. Invite a neurologist, neuropsychologist, or other neuroscientist to class to speak about brain functions and the role of psychological testing in neurology.

2. Bring a plastic three-dimensional model of the brain to class to discuss brain structure and function.

3. With permission and informed consent, invite a head-injured person to class to discuss his/her post-injury experiences, especially as they pertain to psychological testing.

4. Many films and videos provide excellent examples of impaired brain functions. For example, the PBS published two series, The Brain and The Mind. These videos are widely available from various loan libraries.

Essay Questions

1. Summarize the differential functions of the left and right cerebral hemispheres.

2. Discuss the major functions of each of the following cerebral lobes: occipital, temporal, frontal, and parietal. Also, what is the function of the cerebellum?

3. In general, describe and discuss the functions of the ventricles.

4. Describe the major neurobehavioral effects for each of the following conditions: traumatic brain injury, Alzheimer's disease, and stroke.

5. What are some of the symptoms that may occur with temporal lobe dysfunction? [or frontal, parietal, occipital, cerebellar]? What kinds of tests might be designed to detect these symptoms?

TEST ITEM FILE

Topic 9A: A Primer of Neuropsychology

1. According to the text, the impetus for the development of human neuropsychology was
   - a. breakthroughs in medical imaging
   - *b. brain-injured soldiers from WWII
   - c. brain lesions in animals
   - d. none of the above

2. The central nervous system consists of
   - a. the brain
   - *b. the brain and spinal cord
   - c. the brain, spinal cord, and motor nerves
   - d. the brain, spinal cord, motor nerves, and sensory nerves

3. Neurons within the brain reproduce
   - a. up to age three
   - b. up to puberty
   - c. indefinitely
   - *d. not at all

4. In addition to neurons, the brain consists of _____ cells.
   - *a. glial
   - b. somatype
   - c. prion
   - d. none of the above

5. The brain contains more than _____ neurons.
   - a. 100 million
   - *b. 100 billion
   - c. 100 trillion
   - d. 100 quadrillion

6. A single neuron can transmit neural impulses approximately _____ times a second.
   a. 10
   b. 100
   *c. 1,000
   d. 10,000

7. The brain contains a complicated system of fluid-filled caverns called
   *a. ventricles
   b. canals
   c. CSF acquaducts
   d. none of the above

8. Structurally, the lowest brain centers are the most _____ organized.
   *a. simply
   b. complexly
   c. diffusely
   d. none of the above

9. Simple life functions such as breathing are controlled by the
   *a. hindbrain
   b. midbrain
   c. forebrain
   d. none of the above

10. The medulla oblongata is in the
    *a. hindbrain
    b. midbrain
    c. forebrain
    d. none of the above

11. Swallowing is under the control of the
    a. thalamus
    b. frontal lobes
    *c. medulla oblongata
    d. temporal lobes

12. A small stroke in the _____ may cause a partial loss of pain and temperature sense.
    a. lateral geniculate
    b. precentral gyrus
  *c. medulla
    d. cerebellum

13. General arousal and consciousness is governed by the
    a. lateral geniculate
    b. precentral gyrus
  *c. reticular formation
    d. frontal lobes

14. The _____ coordinates the details of automatic, skilled movements.
    a. lateral geniculate
    b. precentral gyrus
    c. medulla
  *d. cerebellum

15. The characteristic wide-based gait found in many chronic alcoholics is a consequence of degeneration in the
    a. lateral geniculate
    b. precentral gyrus
    c. medulla
  *d. cerebellum

16. Many persons diagnosed as autistic possess a small, malformed
    a. lateral geniculate
    b. precentral gyrus
    c. medulla
  *d. cerebellum

17. The superior colliculi are involved in
  *a. vision
    b. audition
    c. touch
    d. movement

18. Cranial nerves are
    a. exclusively sensory
    b. exclusively motor
    c. both sensory and motor
    d. none of the above

19. Most typically, dysfunction of the cranial nerves would be assessed by a
    a. neuropsychologist
    *b. neurologist
    c. psychiatrist
    d. none of the above

20. All sensory information except _____ is relayed through the thalamus.
    a. touch
    b. hearing
    c. vision
    *d. smell

21. Feeding and sexual behavior are governed by the
    a. thalamus
    *b. hypothalamus
    c. amygdala
    d. none of the above

22. The outermost formation of the forebrain is the
    a. diencephalon
    *b. telencephalon
    c. mesencephalon
    d. myelencephalon

23. The regulation of emotion occurs within the
    a. thalamus
    b. hypothalamus
    c. frontal lobe
    *d. limbic lobe

24. The _____ plays a special role in memory
    a. thalamus
    b. hypothalamus
    c. amygdala
    *d. hippocampus

25. Damage to the left hippocampus impairs
    a. vision
    b. spatial thinking
    *c. verbal memory
    d. right-sided movement

26. The basal ganglia are traditionally considered to be part of the
    _____ system.
    a. auditory
    b. visual
    *c. motor
    d. none of the above

27. Parkinson's disease is caused by damage to the
    a. thalamus
    b. hypothalamus
    c. amygdala
    *d. basal ganglia

28. The major commissure that serves to integrate the functions of
the two cerebral hemispheres is the
    a. thalamus
    b. hypothalamus
    *c. corpus callosum
    d. basal ganglia

29. Suppose a patient with a severed corpus callosum has a picture
of an apple presented briefly to the left of the visual fixation point.
What will the patient report seeing?
    *a. "nothing"
    b. "an apple"
    c. "half an apple"
    d. none of the above

30. The prominent bulges in the brain are called
    a. sulci
    b. fissures
    *c. gyri
    d. cortical folds

31. The grooves in the brain are called
    *a. sulci
    b. fissures
    c. gyri
    d. cortical folds

32. Olfactory stimulation in each nostril is processed by
    a. the opposite side of the brain
    *b. the same side of the brain
    c. both sides of the brain
    d. none of the above

33. Vision is processed in the _____ lobe.
    a. frontal
    b. temporal
    *c. occipital
    d. parietal

34. Touch is processed in the _____ lobe.
    a. frontal
    b. temporal
    c. occipital
    *d. parietal

35. Hearing is processed in the _____ lobe.
    a. frontal   c. occipital
    *b. temporal   d. parietal

36. Movement is processed in the _____ lobe.
    *a. frontal
    b. temporal
    c. occipital
    d. parietal

37. A very small lesion in the occipital lobe might produce
   *a. a scotoma
   b. visual tracking problems
   c. blurring in the opposite-sided eye
   d. blurring in the same-sided eye

38. A difficulty in recognizing drawings, objects, or faces is known as a type of
   a. apraxia
   b. alexia
   *c. agnosia
   d. none of the above

39. The postcentral gyrus is in the _____ lobe.
   a. frontal
   b. temporal
   c. occipital
   *d. parietal

40. Damage to the _____ lobe may impair the ability to draw.
   a. frontal
   b. temporal
   c. occipital
   *d. parietal

41. The temporal lobes are involved in
   a. hearing
   b. memory
   c. aggression
   *d. all of the above

42. The perception of nonverbal auditory patterns occurs in the
   a. left temporal lobe
   *b. right temporal lobe
   c. left parietal lobe
   d. right parietal lobe

43. Defects in the delayed recall of pictorial material are linked to damage to the
    a. left temporal lobe
   *b. right temporal lobe
    c. left parietal lobe
    d. right parietal lobe

44. Difficulties perceiving subtle social signals such as discreet but obvious glances at one's watch are linked to damage to the
    a. left temporal lobe
   *b. right temporal lobe
    c. left parietal lobe
    d. right parietal lobe

45. Goal formulation and planning take place especially in the _____ lobes.
   *a. frontal
    b. temporal
    c. occipital
    d. parietal

46. The most common cause of frontal lobe damage is
    a. tumor
    b. drugs
   *c. trauma
    d. none of the above

47. Bilateral frontal lobe damage can lead to
    a. decreased spontaneity
    b. deficits in self-awareness
    c. a concrete attitude
   *d. all of the above

48. Typically, frontal lobe lesions cause _____ in measured IQ.
    a. huge decrements
   *b. little change
    c. marked improvement
    d. unpredictable changes

49. In most persons, language functions are
    *a. lateralized to the left hemisphere
    b. shared equally by both hemispheres
    c. lateralized to the right hemisphere
    d. directly linked to handedness

50. Slow, labored speech is caused by damage to
    a. Wernicke's area
    b. the right parietal lobe
    *c. Broca's area
    d. the left parietal lobe

51. A patient with damage to _____ might respond fluently
"Book, a husbelt, a king of prepator, find it in front of a car ready to be
directed."
    *a. Wernicke's area
    b. the right parietal lobe
    c. Broca's area
    d. the left parietal lobe

52. The connection between Wernicke's and Broca's areas is called
the
    a. corpus callosum   *c. arcuate fasciculus
    b. lateral geniculate   d. lateral tract

53. Damage to the _____ will cause serious reading
disability, but there will be little problem in comprehending speech or
in speaking.
    *a. angular gyrus
    b. lateral geniculate
    c. arcuate fasciculus
    d. lateral tract

54. The impaired ability to deal with spatial relationships either in a
two- or three-dimensional framework is known as
    *a. constructional dyspraxia
    b. dimensional alexia
    c. agnosia
    d. none of the above

55. Diffuse axonal injury is common in
   a. degenerative diseases
   b. alcoholism
   *c. head trauma
   d. cerebrovascular disorders

56. Neuritic plaques and neurofibrillary tangles are common in
   *a. degenerative diseases
   b. alcoholism
   c. head trauma
   d. cerebrovascular disorders

57. Multi-infarct dementia is a form of
   a. degenerative disease
   b. alcoholism
   c. head trauma
   *d. cerebrovascular disorder

58. Atrophy of the mamillary bodies is found in
   a. degenerative diseases   c. head trauma
   *b. alcoholism   d. cerebrovascular disorders

59. This test is especially useful in diagnosing seizure disorders.
   *a. electroencephalography
   b. cerebral angiography
   c. computerized transaxial tomography
   d. positron emission tomography

60. This test is especially useful in detecting an aneurysm.
   a. electroencephalography
   *b. cerebral angiography
   c. computerized transaxial tomography
   d. positron emission tomography

61. This test measures function, not structure.
   a. electroencephalography
   b. cerebral angiography
   c. computerized transaxial tomography
   *d. positron emission tomography

Topic 9B:

Neuropsychological and Geriatric Assessment

A Conceptual Model of Brain-Behavior Relationships

Assessment of Sensory Input

Sensory-perceptual Exam
Finger Localization Test
Other Sensory Measures

Measures of Attention and Concentration

Test of Everyday Attention
Continuous Performance Test
Paced Auditory Serial Addition Task
Subtracting Serial Sevens
Additional Measures of Attentional Impairment

Tests of Learning and Memory

Wechsler Memory Scale-Revised
Rey Auditory Verbal Learning Test
Fuld Object-Memory Evaluation
Additional Tests of Learning and Memory

Assessment of Language Functions

Clinical Examination for Aphasia
Screening and Comprehensive Diagnostic Tests for Aphasia

Tests of Spatial and Manipulatory Ability

Drawing Tests
Assembly Tests

Assessment of Executive Functions

Assessment of Motor Output

Test Batteries in Neuropsychological Assessment

Case Exhibit 9.2: Luria-Nebraska Neuropsychological Battery

Assessment of Mental Status in the Elderly

Mini-Mental State Exam

Summary

Key Terms and Concepts

Classroom Discussion Questions

1. In the assessment of sensory input, why is it important to use both unilateral and simultaneous bilateral stimulation?

2. Discuss the common characteristics of measures of attentional impairment. What do the Continuous Performance Test, subtracting serial sevens, and the Paced Auditory Serial Addition Test have in common?

3. What is aphasia? What are some different symptoms and forms of aphasia? Does anyone in the class know someone with aphasia? What kinds of symptoms does the patient have?

4. Discuss the consequences of frontal lobe injury. What tests might be useful in revealing these neurobehavioral consequences?

5. Have students propose new measures of memory. Discuss how these new measures compare to existing measures such as the WMS-R, Rey Auditory Verbal Learning Test, and Fuld Object Memory Test.

Extramural Assignments

1. Have students find review articles on the reliability and validity of the Luria-Nebraska Neuropsychological Battery. What conclusions do the students derive about this instrument? Written or oral reports might be required.

2. Assign students the task of finding specific examples of aphasic symptoms from the research and clinical literature. Each student could present the symptom to class for discussion.

3. Subtracting serial sevens is a common test for attentional deficit. Have groups of students collect normative data for different normal populations, e.g., college students, community adults, high school students. How commonly do "normal" persons fail this screening test?

4. Require students to find a new neuropsychological test in the research and clinical literature. Have them describe the test and its psychometric characteristics to the class.

Classroom Demonstrations

1. With permission and informed consent, demonstrate the Rey Auditory Verbal Learning Test in class with one or more volunteer subjects. The test is not copyrighted and can be found in Lezak (1995).

2. Invite a speech therapist to class to discuss the role of formal tests in the assessment of aphasia. What are the different forms of aphasia? How can they be assessed, both formally and informally?

3. With permission and informed consent, demonstrate the administration and scoring of the TinkertoyR in class with one or more volunteer subjects. How does this test differ from other more typical measures in neuropsychology? The test can be found in Lezak (1995).

Essay Questions

1. In the assessment of sensory input, why is it important to use both unilateral and simultaneous bilateral stimulation?

2. Define aphasia. List the major types of aphasia and give examples.

3. Describe some commonly used methods for formally assessing attentional deficit.

4. What are the likely consequences of frontal lobe damage? How might these consequences be assessed?

5. What are executive functions? Describe some useful tests of executive functions.

6. Describe the Halstead-Reitan Neuropsychological Battery.

TEST ITEM FILE

Topic 9B: Neuropsychological and Geriatric Assessment

1. An examinee who finds it difficult to process touch in the right hand may have a lesion in the
    a. left precentral gyrus
  *b. left postcentral gyrus
    c. right precentral gyrus
    d. right postcentral gyrus

2. An inability to perceive bilateral simultaneous stimulation may signify the symptom of
    a. collosal interference
    b. blindsight
  *c. suppression
    d. repression

3. The trials of the Benton Finger Localization Test consist of
    a. with the hand visible, identifying single fingers touched by the examiner with the pointed end of a pencil
    b. with the hand hidden from view, identifying single fingers touched by the examiner
    c. with the hand hidden from view, identifying pairs of fingers simultaneously touched by the examiner
    *d. all of the above

4. The purpose of the Von Frey hairs is to determine
    a. the visual acuity of the examinee
    *b. the tactile sensitivity of the examinee
    c. if scotomas exist in the visual field
    d. none of the above

5. For normal subjects, errors on the face-hand test
    *a. are quite rare
    b. are common, but inconsistent
    c. occur only on the simultaneous trials
    d. none of the above

6. Which of the following is a test of attention?
    a. Test of Everyday Attention
    b. Continuous Performance Test
    c. Paced Auditory Serial Addition Test
    *d. all of the above

7. On a modified serial sevens test, how many errors did this subject make: "30, 22, 15, 8, 1"
    a. 0
    *b. 1
    c. 4
    d. none of the above

8. The Continuous Performance Test has been proved sensitive in detecting
    a. hyperactivity
    b. drug effects
    c. schizophrenia
    *d. all of the above

9. If the numbers on the PASAT are "3-1-9-5-4-2" then the examinee should respond
   *a. "4-10-14-9-6"
   b. "4-14-6"
   c. "3-4-13-18-22-24"
   d. none of the above

10. A special application of the PASAT is in the serial testing of
    a. schizophrenics
    b. retarded persons
    *c. concussion patients
    d. school children

11. The Symbol Digit Modalities Test includes
    a. a written trial
    b. an oral trial
    *c. both a written and an oral trial
    d. neither a written nor an oral trial

12. On this test, a voice on the tape might say "freep" while the examinee must read from four choices and underline the correct alternative:
    freeb   fleeb   freep   fleep
    a. Seashore Rhythm Test
    b. Auditory Vigilance Test
    c. Continuous Performance Test
    *d. Speech Sounds Perception Test

13. The standardization sample for the Wechsler Memory Scale-Revised was stratified on the following variable(s):
    a. race   c. education
    b. geographic region   *d. all of the above

14. Recently detoxified alcoholics showed _____ memory deficits on the Wechsler Memory Scale-Revised.
    a. no
    b. mild
    *c. substantial
    d. mysterious

15. The Rey Auditory Verbal Learning Test assesses
    a. short-term memory
    b. long-term memory
    *c. both a and b
    d. neither a nor b

16. The Fuld Object-Memory Evaluation is often used in the assessment of
    a. drug effects
    b. mental retardation
    c. schizophrenia
    *d. Alzheimer's disease

17. A clinical assessment for aphasia would assess
    a. spontaneous speech
    b. word finding
    c. comprehension of language
    *d. all of the above

18. The term _____ refers to a variety of dysfunctions characterized by a breakdown in the direction or execution of complex motor acts.
    a. alexia
    b. agnosia
    c. aphasia
    *d. apraxia

19. Beyond any doubt, the most widely used drawing test is the
    a. Greek Cross
    b. Graham Kendall
    c. House-Tree-Person Test
    *d. Bender Visual Motor Gestalt Test

20. Problems with assembling blocks may indicate dysfunction in the _____ lobe.
    a. frontal
    b. temporal
    *c. parietal
    d. occipital

21. Which of the following is a test of executive functions?
    a. Wisconsin Card Sorting Test
    b. Porteus Mazes
    c. Tinkertoy Test
    *d. all of the above

22. The Porteus Maze Test was originally devised as a
    a. measure of lobotomy effects
    *b. culture-reduced measure of planning and foresight
    c. test for mentally retarded persons
    d. none of the above

23. The Tinkertoy Test is a measure of
    a. constructional skill
    *b. executive functions
    c. problem solving
    d. motor dexterity

24. On the Finger Tapping Test, normative expectation is that the nondominant hand will be about _____ percent of the dominant hand.
    a. 70
    b. 80
    *c. 90
    d. 100

25. On the Finger Tapping Test, the reliability of the ratio score is about
    a. .3
    *b. .5
    c. .7
    d. .9

26. Using the Purdue Pegboard Test in isolation, one study found an ____ percent accuracy in identifying brain impairment among a large group of normal subjects and neurological patients.
    a. 20
    b. 40
    c. 60
    *d. 80

27. This test consists of 269 discrete items.
   *a. Luria-Nebraska Neuropsychological Battery
   b. Halstead-Reitan Neuropsychological Battery
   c. Benton Iowa Battery
   d. none of the above

28. One criticism of the Luria-Nebraska Neuropsychological Battery is that
   a. the standardization sample is too small
   b. the battery takes too long to administer
   *c. scale scores do not quantify specific neuropsychological deficits
   d. all of the above

29. The Halstead-Reitan Neuropsychological Battery includes
   a. Tactual Performance Test
   b. Grip Strength
   c. Seashore Rhythm Test
   *d. all of the above

30. "Put the small red token on top of the blue square" might be a test item on the
   a. Porch Index of Communicative Ability
   *b. Token Test
   c. Boston Diagnostic Aphasia Examination
   d. all of the above

31. When features of a previous stimulus carry over in the current stimulus, the error is called
   a. Collision
   *b. Perseveration
   c. Closure Difficulty
   d. Cohesion

32. Which of the following is a scale on the Luria-Nebraska Neuropsychological Battery?
   a. Rhythm   c. Arithmetic
   b. Reading   *d. all of the above

33. Which of the following is a comprehensive aphasia test?
    a. Aphasia Screening Test
    b. Aphasia Language Performance Scales
    c. Porch Index of Communicative Ability
    *d. Boston Diagnostic Aphasia Examination

34. Which of the following is a memory test?
    a. Complex Figure Test
    b. Facial Recognition Test
    c. Selective Reminding Test
    *d. all of the above

35. The Category Test measures
    *a. abstract reasoning and concept formation
    b. knowledge of categories
    c. mathematical reasoning
    d. maze solving ability

36. The most widely used mental status tool is
    a. Short Portable Mental Status Questionnaire
    b. Mental Status Report
    *c. Mini-Mental State Exam
    d. Mental Status Questionnaire

37. Which of the following is NOT an important component of a typical mental status exam?
    a. thought content
    b. emotional functioning
    *c. psychiatric diagnosis
    d. appearance and behavior

38. One of the more difficult things to evaluate in the mental status exam is:
    *a. insight
    b. orientation
    c. thought content
    d. appearance

Topic 10A

Personnel Assessment and Selection

A Framework For Industrial Testing and Assessment

Key Issues in Personnel Testing
Job Analysis

The Role of Testing in Personnel Selection

Complexities of Personnel Selection
Approaches to Personnel Selection

Autobiographical Data

The Nature of Biodata
The Validity of Biodata

The Employment Interview

Cognitive Ability Tests

Wonderlic Personnel Test
Bennett Mechanical Comprehension Test
Minnesota Clerical Test

Personality and Temperament Tests

Paper-and-Pencil Integrity Tests

Overt Integrity Tests
Personality-based Integrity Tests
Validity of Integrity Tests

Structure and Measurement of Psychomotor Abilities

Taxonomy of Psychomotor Skills

Employee Aptitude Survey
Minnesota Rate of Manipulation Test
Purdue Pegboard

Work Sample and Situational Exercises

The In-Basket Test
Assessment Centers

Summary

Key Terms and Concepts

Classroom Discussion Questions

1. One of the points made in the text is that unstructured interviews constitute a dubious basis for selecting personnel. Ask the students how they would feel about being hired entirely upon the basis of questionnaire data and test scores--no interview.

2. What are the potential advantages of the interview as a job selection device?

3. Ask whether students have taken personality and/or integrity tests as a condition of employment. What were their experiences? Did the tests seem fair, appropriate?

Extramural Assignments

1. Ask groups of students to devise situational exercises for various positions. For example, what would be an appropriate situational exercise for the position of grocery store check-out clerk? Social worker? College instructor?

2. Ask groups of students to survey local businesses and organizations as to how psychological tests are used in personnel

selection. Recommend particularly that students survey law enforcement agencies.

Classroom Demonstrations

1. Demonstrate some tests or simulations of tests used in "blue collar" or clerical personnel selection. For example, the instructor could easily devise a version of the Minnesota Clerical Test. Data from such a test could be compared with other performance measures, both related and unrelated, to show the limitations of such instruments.

2. Administer several overt integrity test items to students. Ask their opinions about the validity of the questions. Examples of items can be obtained from the article by Ryan and Sackett (1987).

Essay Questions

1. Discuss the interview as a personnel selection device.

2. Define work sample and situational exercise. Give a good example of each.

3. Define biodata and give examples. In general, what is the validity of biodata in personnel selection?

4. Discuss the different kinds of integrity tests. What is the validity of these instruments?

TEST ITEM FILE

Topic 10A: Personnel Assessment and Selection

1. The identification of criteria for effective job performance is known as
   a. validational analysis
   *b. job analysis
   c. effectiveness analysis
   d. none of the above

2. Industrial/organizational psychology includes _____
   a. military applications
   b. personnel selection
   c. evaluation of advertising
   *d. all of the above

3. Job analysis consists of
   a. job description
   b. job specification
   *c. both of the above
   d. neither of the above

4. In I/O psychology, DOT stands for
   a. Department of Transportation
   b. Description of Training
   *c. Dictionary of Occupational Titles
   d. Dictionary of Training

5. The Position Analysis Questionnaire contains items that assess
   a. information input
   b. mental processes
   c. personal relationships
   *d. all of the above

6. One concern with the PAQ is that the profile for a police officer
   a. does not capture the reality of the job
   *b. resembles the profile for a housewife
   c. works in metropolitan areas only
   d. has changed substantially since its inception

7. The Job Element Inventory (JEI)
   a. can be completed by the workers themselves
   b. has fewer items than the PAQ
   c. contains the same factors as the PAQ
   *d. all of the above

8. The use of tests for personnel selection is complex because
   *a. job behavior is rarely unidimensional in nature
   b. tests have less validity than is commonly believed
   c. people have become more skilled at faking tests
   d. all of the above

9. According to Guion, research on personnel selection has emphasized
   *a. criterion-related validity
   b. content validity
   c. construct validity
   d. all of the above

10. When comparing the validity of biodata and cognitive ability tests as predictors of training success, a typical finding is
   a. biodata works better than cognitive ability tests
   b. cognitive ability tests work better than biodata
   *c. biodata and cognitive ability tests work about equally well
   d. neither biodata nor cognitive ability tests work very well

11. In the prediction of sales productivity, the average validity coefficient of biodata is about
   a. .2
   b. .4
   *c. .6
   d. .8

12. The identification of criteria for effective job performance is known as   *a. job analysis
   b. employee selection
   c. performance evaluation
   d. all of the above

13. When we use a narrow measure that includes only paper-and-pencil tests, about _____ of the companies in the United States engage in personnel testing.
    a. one-tenth
    b. one-third
    *c. two-thirds
    d. nine-tenths

14. Regarding validity and adverse impact upon minorities, which selection method is best?
    a. self-assessments
    b. reference checks
    c. projective tests
    *d. biodata

15. Suppose skilled interviewers independently interview the same job candidates. The inter-rater reliability of their evaluations will typically be in the
    a. .30s
    *b. .50s
    c. .70s
    d. .90s

16. Suppose skilled interviewers jointly interview the same job candidates using a structured interview schedule. The inter-rater reliability of their evaluations will typically be in the
    a. .30s
    b. .50s
    *c. .70s
    d. .90s

17. The increase in validity when a new source of prediction is added to other sources is known as
    a. predictive validity
    *b. incremental validity
    c. concurrent validity
    d. regression enhancement

18. The persistence of the interview as a method for employee selection is attributed to the following reason(s):
    a. administrators believe the interview is "really" valid in spite of the pessimistic research data
    b. the interview is used in many settings to sell the candidate on the job
    c. the interview may not be valid but practical considerations make it the popular choice
    *d. all of the above

19. A miniature replica of the job for which examinees have applied is called a(n)
    *a. work sample
    b. situational exercise
    c. ergonomic test
    d. none of the above

20. Work samples are especially useful in
    a. professional positions
    b. helping professions
    *c. mechanical trades
    d. none of the above

21. The main difference between a situational exercise and a work sample is that the former
    *a. mirrors only part of the job
    b. duplicates the entire job task
    c. is based upon spontaneous factors
    d. none of the above

22. Which of the following has been developed into a work sample or situational exercise?
    a. a typing test for office personnel
    b. a mechanical assembly test for loom fixers
    c. a map reading test for traffic control officers
    *d. all of the above

23. The classic paper on the in-basket test is the 1962 monograph by
    *a. Frederikson
    b. Samuelson
    c. Landy
    d. Schmidt

24. Effective action by administrators consists of
    a. preparing for action
    b. amount of work
    c. not needing guidance
    *d. all of the above

25. When scored on the in-basket technique, undergraduates stressed
    a. control over subordinates
    b. concern for outsiders
    *c. verbal productivity
    d. all of the above

26. A recent study of the in-basket technique by Brannick and others (1989) found
    *a. low correlations on the subscales from two in-basket forms
    b. strong support for the construct validity of the method
    c. excellent construct validity for managerial positions only
    d. all of the above

27. Except for work samples, the most valid selection method for entry-level jobs is
    *a. an appropriate ability test
    b. a structured interview
    c. a structured questionnaire
    d. none of the above

28. For entry-level jobs, the mean validity coefficient for ability tests is about
    a. .34
    *b. .54
    c. .74
    d. .94

29. The Wonderlic Personnel Test is a group test of
    a. clerical skill
    b. job honesty
    c. interpersonal skills
    *d. general mental ability

30. The Wonderlic Personnel Test comes in
    a. a single form that is updated every two years
    *b. numerous parallel forms
    c. three versions for ages 19-24, 25-40, and 40+
    d. none of the above

31. Reliability of the Wonderlic Personnel Test is typically around
    a. .50
    b. .60
    c. .80
    *d. .90

32. Normative data for the Wonderlic Personnel Test are based upon
    _____ subjects.
    a.   50
    b.   500
    c.   5,000
    *d. 50,000

33. Race differences on the Wonderlic Personnel Test are
    a. nonexistent
    b. trivial
    *c. significant
    d. unknown

34. This test proved to be one of the best predictors of pilot success
during World War II.
    a. Wonderlic Personnel Test
    *b. Bennett Mechanical Comprehension Test
    c. Minnesota Clerical Test
    d. Strong Vocational Interest Blank

35. The Bennett Mechanical Comprehension Tests consists of
    a. "hands on" test items such as fixing a rachet
    b. a multiple choice section based upon tool knowledge
    *c. pictures about which the examinee must answer straightforward questions
    d. all of the above

36. The Minnesota Clerical Test consists of
    a. number comparison   *c. both a and b
    b. name comparison   d. neither a nor b

37. The score on the Minnesota Clerical Test consists of
    a. total number of items answered
    b. total number of items answered correctly
    *c. total number of items answered correctly minus the number of errors
    d. none of the above

38. A significant concern about the Minnesota Clerical Test is that
    *a. the norm groups are vaguely specified
    b. the reliability is questionable, on the order of .50
    c. both a and b
    d. neither a nor b

39. One problem with the early application of personality tests to personnel selection was that
    *a. there was no established relation between test scores and job success
    b. legal barriers prevented I/O psychologists from using appropriate tests
    c. existing tests did not possess sufficient validity to be used for personnel selection
    d. none of the above

40. An overt integrity test assesses
    a. attitudes toward theft
    b. beliefs about extent of employee theft
    c. degree of condemnation of theft
    *d. all of the above

41. The text points out a serious problem with overt integrity tests:
    a. ethical constraints curtail their use
    b. past behavior does not necessarily predict future behavior
    *c. apparently, they are easily faked
    d. none of the above

42. A serious problem with most integrity tests is the very high fail rate, typically in the _____ range.
    a. 10 percent to 30 percent
    *b. 30 percent to 60 percent
    c. 50 percent to 80 percent
    d. 70 percent to 90 percent

43. Fleishman and other researchers have identified approximately _____ different ability factors in the psychomotor domain
    a. 5
    b. 10
    c. 15
    *d. 20

44. The Purdue Pegboard test is a measure of
    a. gross movement of hands, fingers, and arms
    b. fingertip dexterity
    *c. both of the above
                d. neither of the above

Topic 10B

Appraisal of Work Performance

Functions of Performance Appraisal

Approaches to Performance Appraisal

    Personnel Data: Absenteeism
    Peer Ratings and Self-Assessments
    Supervisor Rating Scales

Sources of Error in Performance Appraisal

    Halo Effect
    Rater Bias
    Criterion Contamination
    Guidelines for Performance Appraisal

Legal Issues in I/O Assessment

    Early Court Cases and Legislation
    Advent of EEOC Employment Testing Standards
    Uniform Guidelines on Employee Selection
    Legal Implications of Subjective Employment Devices
    Recent Developments in Employee Selection

Summary

Key Terms and Concepts

Classroom Discussion Questions

1. Most students have some work experience. Ask them whether the absenteeism of other workers was ever a good basis for performance evaluation.

2. Almost everyone has received an evaluation from a supervisor. Ask students to describe various rating systems and to discuss their

perceptions of the accuracy and fairness of different approaches to performance evaluation.

Extramural Assignments

1. Ask students to collect samples of rating scales used for performance evaluation. For example, they might approach local businesses to determine what instruments are used to evaluate employees. Have the students bring these scales to class for purposes of discussion.

2. Assign students the task of developing a behaviorally anchored rating scale for "examination study behavior."

Classroom Demonstrations

1. Pick a specific work domain such as cook at a fast food restaurant. Ask students to develop rating scales of various kinds in class and submit them to the instructor. In turn, the instructor could render each on overhead projector for purposes of general classroom discussion.

Essay Questions

1. Give examples of three different kinds of rating scales.

2. What is a behaviorally anchored rating scale? Give examples.

3. What is a halo effect? Describe several approaches to control for halo effects.

4. Describe several approaches to improving performance appraisal systems.

TEST ITEM FILE

Topic 10B: Appraisal of Work Performance

1. Adverse impact exists if one group has a selection rate less than _____ the rate of the group with the highest selection rate.
   - a. two-fifths
   - b. three-fifths
   - *c. four-fifths
   - d. nine-tenths

2. Performance evaluation serves the following common use(s)
   - a. determine organizational training needs
   - b. document personnel decisions
   - c. meet legal requirements
   - *d. all of the above

3. The problems encountered in performance evaluation are usually referred to as the _____ problem.
   - a. normative
   - b. evaluative
   - c. predictor
   - d. criterion

4. In general, for assessing the effectiveness of employees,
   - a. objective methods are common and practical
   - *b. judgmental methods are often the only practical approach
   - c. self-assessments work best
   - d. none of the above

5. Although production counts are a desirable method for assessing employee effectiveness, they suffer from the following problem(s):
   - a. the rate of productivity may not be under the control of the worker
   - b. production counts are not applicable to most jobs
   - c. an emphasis upon production counts may distort the quality of the output
   - *d. all of the above

6. The position of the text is that, in general, absenteeism is
   a. an effective and valuable index of of work performance
   *b. a largely useless measure of work performance
   c. a valuable index only for workers who are rarely absent
   d. none of the above

7. In developing a behaviorally anchored rating scale, experts are used to
   a. identify and define performance dimensions
   b. generate behavior examples
   c. scale the behaviors meaningfully
   *d. all of the above

8. The process of developing a behaviorally anchored rating scale may have the indirect benefit of
   *a. identifying the components of effective performance
   b. causing management and labor to see each other's viewpoint
   c. improving the accuracy of employee selection
   d. all of the above

9. This method of performance evaluation has never really caught on.
   a. critical-incidents checklist
   b. behaviorally-anchored rating scale
   *c. forced-choice scale
   d. graphic scale

10. The tendency to rate an employee high or low on all dimensions because of a global impression is called
    *a. halo effect
    b. rater bias
    c. criterion contamination
    d. none of the above

11. A leniency error, as when the supervisor wants to be liked by everyone, is an example of
    a. halo effect   c. criterion contamination
    *b. rater bias   d. none of the above

12. When an evaluation includes factors that are not demonstrably part of the job, this is known as
    a. halo effect
    b. rater bias
    *c. criterion contamination
    d. none of the above

13. The stipulation that medical tests may not be administered prior to an offer of employment was part of the
    a. Civil Rights Act of 1991
    *b. Americans with Disabilities Act of 1990
    c. Uniform Guidelines on Employee Selection of 1978
    d. all of the above

14. The first involvement of the courts in employment testing was
    *a. Myart v. Motorola   c. Albemarle v. Moody
    b. Griggs v. Duke Power   d. none of the above

15. As a consequence of Watson v. Fort Worth Bank and Trust, employers
    a. won the right to use interviews as a selection device
    b. were told to use objective tests only in the selection process
    *c. were warned that subjective selection devices such as interview must be validated
    d. none of the above

16. By far, the most common approach to performance appraisal is
    a. measures of productivity
    b. peer ratings
    *c. supervisor rating scales
    d. subjective evaluation of supervisors

17. This approach consists of trait labels, brief definitions of the labels, and a continuum for the rating.
    *a. graphic rating scale
    b. behavior observation scale
    c. forced-choice scale
    d. critical-incidents checklist

18. The following approach(es) has/have been recommended to control for halo effect:
   a. supervise the supervisors during the rating
   b. practice simulations before doing the ratings
   c. provide supeervisors with a short lecture on halo
   *d. all of the above

19. An example of _____ bias is when one salesperson is assigned to a wealthy neighborhood and others must seek sales in isolated, rural areas.
   *a. opportunity   c. knowledge of predictor bias
   b. group-characteristic   d. supervisor

20. An example of _____ bias is when workers in the same unit agree to limit their productivity to maintain positive social relations.
   a. opportunity
   *b. group-characteristic
   c. knowledge of predictor bias
   d. supervisor

21. An example of _____ bias is when a supervisor permits personal knowledge about an employee to bias the appraisal.
   a. opportunity
   b. group-characteristic
   *c. knowledge of predictor bias
   d. supervisor

22. This act outlaws subgroup norming of employee selection tests.
   a. Uniform Guidelines on Employee Selection
   b. Americans with Disabilities Act
   *c. Civil Rights Act of 1991
   d. none of the above

23. This court case was unique because it pertained to the value and validity of individual test items as opposed to overall test scores.
   a. Myart v. Motorola
   b. Griggs v. Duke Power
   c. Washington v. Davis
   *d. Soraka v. Dayton Hudson

Topic 11A

Assessment of Interests and Values

An Overview of Interest Assessment

Strong Interest Inventory (SII)

   Origins and Assumptions of the SVIB
   The Strong Interest Inventory (SII)
   Evaluation of the SII

Jackson Vocational Interest Survey (JVIS)

Kuder General Interest Survey

   The Kuder General Interest Survey
   Comment on the KGIS and Other Interest Inventories

Vocational Preference Inventory

   Validity of the VPI

Self-Directed Search

   Validity of the Self-Directed Search

Campbell Interest and Skill Survey

The Assessment of Values

   Study of Values
   Rokeach Value Survey
   Limitations of the Rokeach Values Survey
   Values Inventory

The Assessment of Moral Judgement

The Moral Judgment Scale
Stages of Moral Development
Critique of the Moral Judgment Scale
The Defining Issues Test

Summary

Key Terms and Concepts

Classroom Discussion Questions

1. A useful discussion question is for students to compare and contrast the characteristics of the major interest inventories. How are the Strong Interest Inventory, Jackson Vocational Interest Blank, Kuder General Interest Survey, and Campbell Interest and Skills Survey similar and dissimilar?

2. Is it really realistic to separate moral reasoning from specific moral codes of right and wrong, as Kohlberg does in his theory of moral development? Wouldn't most persons at higher stages of moral reasoning tend to propose similar solutions to the moral dilemmas posed by Kohlberg?

Extramural Assignments

1. Have students collect responses to Kohlberg's moral dilemmas (which are widely published in many personality, developmental, and introductory textbooks) and try to analyze, in writing, the stages represented by those responses.

2. Using the RIASEC model (discussed in the text) have students attempt to categorize themselves and others as to personality and work type. Does the model seem to work?

3. Require students to read and summarize reviews of prominent interest inventories from the Mental Measurements Yearbook and/or Test Critique series.

Classroom Demonstrations

1. An interesting demonstration is to have students write anonymous responses to one or more of Kohlberg's moral dilemmas. Then, the instructor and class members can attempt to determine the corresponding stage of moral development for individual responses.

2. Outline the RIASEC model on the blackboard or overhead transparency. Then, describe particular vocations and ask students to identify the corresponding type.

3. Invite a counseling psychologist to class to speak about the value of interest tests in vocational guidance. Student counseling centers at most universities employ one or more such persons.

Essay Questions

1. Describe the guiding assumptions used in the development of the Strong Interest Inventory.

2. Discuss the Kuder General Interest Survey. What age groups are appropriate for its use? What is the structure of the test? What about reliability and validity evidence?

3. Describe and discuss the seven primary Orientations of the Campbell Interest and Skill Survey.

4. What is the evidence for the validity of Kohlberg's Moral Judgment Scale?

TEST ITEM FILE

Topic 11A: Assessment of Interests and Values

1. The first edition of the Strong Vocational Interest Blank appeared
in   a. 1907   c. 1947
       *b. 1927   d. 1967

2. The first edition of the Strong Vocational Interest Blank used
_____ for scale construction.
    a. rational item assignment
    b. factor analysis
    *c. empirical keying
    d. none of the above

3. The development of the Strong Vocational Interest Blank was
based upon the following assumption(s):
    a. each occupation has a desirable pattern of interests and
personality characteristics among its workers
    b. individuals have relatively stable interests and personality
traits
    c. individuals in given occupations differ from one another in
traits and interests
    *d. all of the above

4. The latest version of the Strong Interest Inventory incorporates the
following feature(s):
    a. men's and women's forms are merged into a single edition
    b. a theoretical framework guides the interpretation of scores
    c. an increase in the number of vocational/technical scales
    *d. all of the above

5. Which of the following is NOT a general occupational theme on
the Strong Interest Inventory?
    a. Realistic
    b. Investigative
    c. Artistic
    *d. Scientific

6. Which of the following is a Basic Interest Scale on the Strong Interest Inventory?
   a. Realistic
   b. Investigative
   c. Artistic
   *d. Adventure

7. On the Strong Interest Inventory, one- and two-week stability coefficients for the occupational scales are generally in the
   a. .30s
   b. .50s
   c. .70s
   *d. .90s

8. For respondents over age 25 when first tested, ten to twenty year test-retest correlations for the Strong Interest Inventory occupational scales are generally in the
   a. .20s
   b. .40s
   c. .60s
   *d. .80s

9. Strong (1955) reported that the chances were about _____ that people would be in occupations predicted by high occupational scale scores.
   a. one in five
   b. two in five
   *c. two in three
   d. nine in ten

10. Strong (1955) reported that the chances were about _____ that respondents would be in occupations for which they had shown little interest when tested.
    a. one in one hundred
    b. one in twenty
    *c. one in five
    d. one in two

11. The Strong Interest Inventory is used mainly with
    *a. high school and college students
    b. clients in counseling centers
    c. armed services recruits
    d. psychiatric patients

12. The Jackson Vocational Interest Survey consists of
    a. work role scales
    b. work style scales
    *c. both a and b
    d. neither a nor b

13. The response format for the Jackson Vocational Interest Survey consists of
    a. like-indifferent-dislike
    b. true-false
    *c. forced-choice
    d. all of the above

14. Scale construction for the Jackson Vocational Interest Survey was
    a. rational
    b. theory-guided
    *c. both a and b
    d. neither a nor b

15. The Jackson Vocational Interest Survey takes about _____ to complete.
    a. ten minutes
    b. one-half hour
    *c. one hour
    d. two hours

16. Scale scores on the Jackson Vocational Interest Survey are normed with an average of _____ and a standard deviation of _____.
    *a. 30, 10
    b. 50, 10
    c. 100, 10
    d. 100, 15

17. The target population for the Kuder General Interest Survey is
  a. adults age 16 and over
  b. adults age 21 and over
  *c. adolescents in grades 6 through 12
  d. adolescents in grades 10 through 12

18. The format for the Kuder General Interest Survey consists of
  *a. forced-choice triads   c. multiple choice
  b. forced-choice pairs   d. true-false

19. The format for the Kuder General Interest Survey is particularly suited to
  a. testing examinees with low intelligence
  *b. identifying examinees who have not answered the items sincerely
  c. both a and b
  d. neither a nor b

20. Which of the following scales is found on the Kuder General Interest Survey?
  a. Literary
  b. Musical
  c. Social Service
  *d. all of the above

21. A major problem with all existing interest inventories is that they pay too little attention to
  a. the role of traits in vocational interest
  b. the diversity of possible job roles
  *c. the role of opportunity in job choice
  d. all of the above

22. This test consists of 160 occupational titles toward which the examinee expresses a feeling by markilng Y (yes) or N (no).
  a. Strong Interest Inventory
  b. Campbell Interest and Skill Survey
  *c. Vocational Preference Inventory
  d. Kuder General Interest Scale

23. Most likely, the Holland code of RSE would correspond to:
    a. mathematics teacher
    b. secretary
    c. police officer
    *d. taxi driver

24. Most likely, the Holland code of CSA would correspond to:
    a. mathematics teacher
    *b. secretary
    c. police officer
    d. taxi driver

25. Most likely, the Holland code of ISC would correspond to:
    *a. mathematics teacher
    b. secretary
    c. police officer
    d. taxi driver

26. The Self-Directed Search is designed to be
    a. self-administered
    b. self-scored
    *c. both a and b
    d. neither a nor b

27. The hand-scored version of the Self-Directed Search is prone to
about a _____ percent error rate when scored by high school
students.
    a. 6
    *b. 16
    c. 36
    d. 56

28. The Self-Directed Search is based on
    a. Strong's typology of vocational interests
    *b. Holland's hexagonal model of general occupational themes
    c. Campbell's theory of vocational choice
    d. all of the above

29. In occupational themes, which type is masculine?
    a. Investigative
    b. Enterprising
    c. Conventional
    *d. Realistic

30. In occupational themes, which type fits well in scientific positions?
    *a. Investigative
    b. Enterprising
    c. Conventional
    d. Realistic

31. In occupational themes, which type has good selling skills?
    a. Investigative
    *b. Enterprising
    c. Conventional
    d. Realistic

32. Scores on the Investigative and Enterprising themes show
    _____ correlations.
    a. strong and positive
    b. weak and positive
    *c. negligible
    d. strong and negative

33. Influencing, Organizing, and Helping are Orientation scales on the
    a. Strong Interest Inventory
    *b. Campbell Interest and Skill Survey
    c. Vocational Preference Inventory
    d. Kuder General Interest Scale

34. On the Campbell Interest and Skill, the average score on
Accountant by accountants is:
    a. 120
    b. 100
    *c. 75
    d. 50

35. The Study of Values measured all of the following evaluative attitudes EXCEPT
   a. theoretical
   b. economic
   c. aesthetic
   *d. athletic

36. All of the following are terminal values on the Rokeach Values Survey, EXCEPT:
   a. an exciting life
   b. a comfortable life
   *c. broadminded
   d. pleasure

37. In scoring Kohlberg's Moral Judgment Scale, the examiner pays primary attention to
   a. the choices preferred in moral dilemmas
   *b. the reasons given for moral choices
   c. the logical coherence of the entire test protocol
   d. none of the above

38. Research findings suggest that the Moral Judgment Scale is
   a. reliable
   b. internally consistent
   c. theory consistent
   *d. all of the above

39. Scoring on the Defining Issues Test is
   a. based entirely upon the informed judgment of the examiner
   b. based partly upon the informed judgment of the examiner
   *c. completely objective
   d. both b and c

Topic 11B

Work Values, Career, and Consumer Assessment

Assessment of Work Values and Career Development

Minnesota Importance Questionnaire
Work Values Inventory
Values Scale
Assessment of Career Development

Integrative Model of Career Assessment

Ability Patterns in Career Assessment
Synthesis: The Integrative Model of Career Assessment

Consumer Assessment

Telephone Surveys
Mail Surveys
Focus Groups
Psychophysiological Measurement

Summary

Key Terms and Concepts

Classroom Discussion Questions

1. Ask students to discuss whether they and/or their parents actually enjoy their work. If not, is this because of a clash between personal values and values inherent to specific jobs?

2. Discuss the ethics of telephone surveys. Are there any issues with respect to invasion of privacy?

Extramural Assignments

1. Assign students the task of interviewing their parents and relatives with respect to work values and personal values. What values appear to be inherent to the jobs discussed? Students should prepare a brief summary of their impressions and findings, using concepts from the textbook.

Classroom Demonstrations

1. Select a small group of students and conduct a focus group with them in front of the rest of the class. A possible topic for discussion might be: What makes a "self-help" book a good seller?

Essay Questions

1. Describe and discuss the format of the Minnesota Importance Questionnaire.

2. Describe and discuss the integrative model of career assessment.

3. What are the best conditions for conducting a telephone survey?

4. In consumer psychology, what is the value of pupillary constriction?

TEST ITEM FILE

Topic 11B: Work Values, Career, and Consumer Assessment

1. Studs Terkel concluded that most people _____ their work.
   a. like
   b. tolerate
   *c. dislike
   d. hate

2. The Minnesota Importance Questionnaire attempts to measure ___ needs.
   - *a. 20
   - b. 100
   - c. 190
   - d. 210

3. The Minnesota Importance Questionnaire is interpreted in reference to
   - a. normative data for the general population
   - *b. occupational reinforcer patterns
   - c. rationally derived profiles
   - d. empirically derived profiles

4. In answering items on the Work Values Inventory, the subject
   - a. chooses yes-no
   - *b. marks on a 5-point continuum
   - c. chooses like, dislike, or no preference
   - d. none of the above

5. The integrative model of career assessment makes use of information about
   - a. interests
   - b. abillity
   - c. personality
   - *d. all of the above

6. The preferred approach to surveying is the
   - a. mail questionnaire
   - b. door-to-door questionnaire
   - *c. telephone survey
   - d. business survey

7. The purpose of random digit dialing is to
   - a. speed up the process of telephone surveying
   - *b. control for unlisted numbers
   - c. provide a stratified random sample of the population
   - d. none of the above

8. The most serious problem with mail surveys is
   *a. low return rate
   b. poor representation of the population
   c. cost
   d. designing an effective questionnaire

9. Focus groups feature
   a. interaction of the participants
   b. presence of a moderator
   *c. both a and b
   d. neither a nor b

10. Pupillary response was first popularized as an assessment method by
   a. Pavlov
   b. Freud
   c. Strong
   *d. Hess

11. Recent research indicates that
   *a. the pupil dilates to interesting stimuli
   b. the pupil constricts to unpleasant stimuli
   c. both a and b
   d. neither a nor b

12. What is the current status of physiological measures as they apply to marketing applications?
   a. these measures have been demonstrated as invalid for marketing purposes
   *b. validation studies of physiological measures are lacking
   c. physiological measures have been proven valid for marketing purposes
   d. none of the above

13. Improving the efficiency of mail surveys can be accomplished by
   a. providing advance notice
   b. sending the questionnaire by stamped mail
   c. providing a return envelope
   *d. all of the above

Topic 12A

Assessment of the Environment

Historical Origins of Environmental Assessment

Pioneers of Environmental Psychology
Assessment of the Physical Environment: An Example

Social Climate Scales of Rudolph Moos

Background and Description
Focus Upon the Family Environment Scale
Technical Features
Practical Applications and Uses

In Brief: Two Additional Measures of Social Climate

Home Observation for Measurement of the Environment (HOME)

Backgrond and Description
Technical Features
Practical Applications and Uses

Summary

Key Terms and Concepts

Classroom Discussion Questions

1. Ask students to discuss how they might assess physical environments well known to them, e.g., library, student union building, local bus depot, etc. Certainly the students will be able to discuss differences in a qualitative way, but be sure to ask them how they would *quantify* these aspects of environments.

2. Ask students to discuss how they might assess social environments well known to them, e.g., fraternities, sororities,

dormitories. Certainly the students will be able to discuss differences in a qualitative way, but be sure to ask them how they would *quantify* these aspects of environments.

Extramural Assignments

1. Circulate the Thompson et al. (1990) article, which lists items on the home-likeness scale. Then, ask students to evaluate different locations, e.g., student commons area, dormitories, fraternities, etc.

2. Assign students the task of finding a recent article using one of the Moos Social Climate Scales. Ask students to summarize the article and its findings in one page or less.

Classroom Demonstrations

1. Obtain copies of the Classroom Environment Scale (CES) of Rudolph Moos. Ask students to fill it out anonymously. After scoring the tests, report average scores during a later class period.

Essay Questions

1. What is meant by the tautological problem in environmental assessment?

2. Define social climate and give examples.

3. Give examples of five or six items from the Home Observation for the Measurement of Environment.

4. List five of the social climate scales published by Rudolph Moos.

TEST ITEM FILE

Topic 12A: Assessment of the Environment

1. Which of the following is an example of environment?
   a. noise from physical surroundings
   b. nutritional value of food
   c. stimulation received from parents
   *d. all of the above

2. The idea that variations in our surroundings are the primary source of individual differences is the _____ position.
   *a. environmentalist
   b. nativist
   c. psychodynamic
   d. humanistic

3. The necessity of defining environment independent of behavior is known as the _____ problem.
   a. nativist
   b. empiricist
   *c. tautological
   d. environmental

4. _____ are defined by location, agenda, participants, and scheduling.
   *a. Behavior settings
   b. Environments
   c. Developmental epochs
   d. Social settings

5. An example of a behavior setting would be a(n)
   a. spontaneous riot
   b. library study table
   *c. Boy Scout troop
   d. all of the above

6. Barker, one of the pioneers of environmental psychology, catalogued a total of ___ behavior settings.
   a. 20
   b. 40
   c. 80
   *d. 120

7. Which profession has led the way in the assessment of the environment?
   - *a. architecture
   - b. engineering
   - c. law
   - d. psychology

8. The Social Climate Scales were authored by
   - a. Barker
   - b. Craik
   - *c. Moos
   - d. Skinner

9. Social Climate Scales have been developed for
   - a. families
   - b. student living groups
   - c. military environments
   - *d. all of the above

10. The Ward Atmosphere Scale was initially developed in treatment settings for
   - a. chronic medical problems
   - *b. alcoholism
   - c. jails
   - d. all of the above

11. Which of the below is a subscale on the Family Environment Scale?
   - a. Cohesion
   - b. Conflict
   - c. Independence
   - *d. all of the above

12. Studies of family therapy with the Family Environment Scale have indicated increases on which scale(s)?
   - a. Cohesion
   - b. Expressiveness
   - c. Independence
   - *d. all of the above

13. Traditional measures of social class usually rely upon
    a. occupation
    b. place of residence
    c. education
    *d. all of the above

14. The HOME scale relies upon
    *a. direct observation of the children's home
    b. parental ratings on 27 variables
    c. knowledge of occupation, residence, and education
    d. none of the above

15. The correlations between HOME scores at 12 months and IQ at 54 months were about
    a. .1
    b. .3
    *c. .5
    d. .7

16. The HOME is available in _____ form(s).
    a. 1
    b. 2
    *c. 3
    d. 4

17. One problem with the HOME is that the standardization samples contain ___ African-American families.
    a. no
    b. too few
    *c. too many
    d. an unknown percentage of

18. Completion of the HOME inventory takes about
    a. 10 minutes
    *b. 1 hour
    c. 3 hours day
    d. 1 day

Topic 12B

Person-Environment Assessment

Interactional Approach: Definition

Interactional Assessment: Historical Overview

Transactional Analysis of Personality and Environment

> Background to TAPE: Semantic Differential
> Validity of TAPE

Person-Environment Theory: The Holland Approach

> Theory of Personality Types and Work Environments
> Basic Assumptions of the Holland Approach

Summary

Key Terms and Concepts

Classroom Discussion Questions

1. Ask students to discuss how they would rate their campus (1 to 11) on theTAPE dimensions of authoritarian-democratic, grinding-funloving, religious-secular, idealistic-materialistic, egalitarian-status oriented.

2. Ask students to rate themselves on the traits that correspond to the personality-environment types of Holland (p. 492). Based upon these ratings, have them summarize their personalities by the three highest letters, e.g., RIA for Realistic, Investigative, and Artistic. Do these ratings appear to have any validity?

Extramural Assignment

1. Have students develop their own TAPE-like semantic differential (see Discussion question #1, above). The students could then administer this instrument to a representative sample of students at their institution and report average scores.

Classroom Demonstration

1. Develop your own TAPE-like semantic differential (see Discussion question #1, above). Administer the scale to students in the class and discuss the findings.

Essay Questions

1. Describe the fundamental assumptions and characteristics of the interactional approach to assessment.

2. What is a semantic differential? What are the three major factors of this instrument?

3. Define and describe the six personality types of Holland's theory.

TEST ITEM FILE

Topic 12B: Person-Environment Assessment

1. According to interactional psychologists, individual development is
   a. dynamic
   b. continuous
   c. reciprocal
   *d. all of the above

2. The idea that person and environment should be viewed as a single constellation is
   a. integration
   *b. field
   c. differentiation
   d. nativism

3. The theory of needs and press was first promoted by
   *a. Murray
   b. Stern
   c. Holland
   d. Pervin

4. The twin measure to the Activities Index was the
   a. Climate Score
   b. Thought Index
   c. Cohort Index
   *d. College Characteristics Index

5. An approach to measuring the connotative meaning of concepts is
   *a. semantic differential
   b. transactional analysis
   c. needs/press theory
   d. none of the above

6. Factor analyses of the semantic differential usually reveal ___ major factor(s).
   a. one   *c. three
   b. two   d. four

7. The central assumption of _____ is that a "fit" between personal characteristics and college characteristics is essential for student satisfaction.
    *a. Transactional Analysis of Personality and Environment
    b. College Characteristics Index
    c. Vocational Preference Inventory
    d. Institutional Functioning Inventory

8. The acronym RIASEC is associated with whose theory?
    a. Murray
    b. Pervin
    *c. Holland
    d. none of the above

9. Which of the following theorists believed that interest inventories are, essentially, personality inventories?
    a. Murray
    b. Pervin
    *c. Holland
    d. none of the above

10. Holland's Self-Directed Search asks for input about
    a. activities
    b. competencies
    c. occupations
    *d. all of the above

11. Satisfaction in college environments is best predicted by
    a. assessment of the person
    b. assessment of the environment
    *c. assessment of the person-environment fit
    d. none of the above

Topic 13A

Theories and the Measurement of Personality

Personality: An Overview

Psychoanalytic Theories of Personality

  Origins of Psychoanalytic Theory
  The Structure of the Mind
  The Role of Defense Mechanisms
  Assessment of Defense Mechanisms and Ego Functions

Type Theories of Personality

  Type A Coronary-Prone Behavior Pattern

Phenomenological Theories of Personality

  Origins of the Phenomenological Approach
  Carl Rogers, Self Theory, and the Q-Technique

Behavioral and Social Learning Theories

Trait Conceptions of Personality

  Cattell's Factor-Analytic Trait Theory
  Eysenck's Trait-Dimensional Theory
  The Five-Factor Model of Personality
  Critique of the Trait Concept

Summary

Key Terms and Concepts

Classroom Discussion Questions

1. What is personality? A good starting point for this topic is to ask students to express their understandings of the term "personality."

2. Is it possible to verify a theory such as psychoanalysis? In particular, what specific predictions flow from psychoanalytic theory which can be tested in the real world?

3. What characteristics do defense mechanisms have in common? What are some of the more common defense mechanisms? Can students cite examples from their own or other's lives of defense mechanisms in action?

4. What are the characteristics of Type A behavior? Can students cite examples of Type A behavior in their own or other's lives?

5. Compare and contrast major personality theories, e.g., Cattell, Eysenck, Costa and McCrae, and Rogers.

Extramural Assignments

1. Ask groups of students to develop their own Q-sort for personality. Have them examine the interrater agreement when the same person is evaluated with the Q-sort by two or more judges.

2. One point made by the textbook is that personality constructs rarely exceed predictive validity coefficients of .30. Ask students to search the journal literature for examples of the predictive validity of personality constructs. Does Mischel's pessimistic conclusion still hold true?

3. Request that students read Vaillant's (1977) Adaptation to Life. This is a fascinating book, rich with clinical detail, that expresses the psychoanalytic viewpoint very clearly.

Classroom Demonstrations

1. Some students have difficulty conceptualizing the use of the Q-sort. A miniature Q-sort could be developed and each student could be required, in class, to sort the cards for self, the instructor, a parent, or friend.

2. An interesting way to generate discussion on defense mechanisms is to have students fill out a sentence completion form, and then analyze responses, anonymously, for the presence of defense mechanisms.

3. Portray the 20 dimensions of Cattell's 16PF on blackboard or overhead transparency and ask students to rate themselves or others on each dimension. This is an active form of learning which should promote retention regarding the nature of Cattell's instrument.

Essay Questions

1. Define personality. Is personality a useful construct? Why or why not.

2. Outline the major tenets of the psychoanalytic view on personality.

3. What is a defense mechanism? Name three prominent defense mechanisms and cite examples of each.

4. What is Type A behavior? Is it a useful construct? Why or why not?

5. Outline the major tenet's of Roger's [or Cattell's, or Eysenck's, or Costa and McCrae's] view on personality.

TEST ITEM FILE

Topic 13A: Theories and the Measurement of Personality

1. The construct of personality is difficult to define, but includes the following distinctive feature(s):
   - a. consistency
   - b. distinctiveness
   - *c. both a and b
   - d. neither a nor b

2. The position of the textbook is that personality and intelligence are
   - a. indistinguishable
   - *b. separate but intertwined constructs
   - c. separate and distinct
   - d. none of the above

3. Which of the following personality tests has a significant loading on intelligence?
   - a. MMPI
   - b. CPI
   - *c. 16 PF
   - d. none of the above

4. Freud began his professional career as a
   - a. psychiatrist
   - b. psychologist
   - *c. neurologist
   - d. gynecologist

5. According to Freud, abreaction is a
   - *a. release of emotion
   - b. buried memory
   - c. hysterical reaction
   - d. partial paralysis

6. Hysteria may be characterized by
   - a. histrionic behavior
   - b. loss of sensation
   - c. apparent paralysis
   - *d. all of the above

7. Freud believed that the _____ was a reservoir of instinctual drives.
   a. preconscious
   b. libido
   *c. unconscious
   d. none of the above

8. According to Freud, the ____ is the obscure and inaccessible part of our personality.
   *a. id
   b. ego
   c. superego
   d. none of the above

9. The id is
   *a. entirely unconscious
   b. partly unconscious and partly conscious
   c. entirely conscious
   d. unconscious in sleep, conscious in daytime

10. The _____ operates in accordance with the pleasure-principle.
    *a. id
    b. ego
    c. superego
    d. libido

11. The _____ operates in accordance with the reality-principle.
    a. id
    *b. ego
    c. superego
    d. libido

12. According to Freud, time and logic are irrelevant to the
    *a. id
    b. superego
    c. id and superego
    d. none of the above

13. According to Freud, the ego develops
    a. on its own
    *b. from the id
    c. from the superego
    d. none of the above

14. The superego is
    a. entirely unconscious
    *b. partly conscious and partly unconscious
    c. entirely conscious
    d. conscious in sleep, unconscious in the daytime

15. The main weapon of the superego is
    a. altruism
    *b. guilt
    c. logic
    d. threat

16. All defense mechanisms share the following characteristic(s):
    a. they reduce anxiety
    b. they operate unconsciously
    c. they distort reality
    *d. all of the above

17. The use of defense mechanisms is
    a. always counterproductive
    *b. undesirable when excessive and rigid
    c. always desirable
    d. none of the above

18. The delineation of defense mechanisms was left to Freud's followers, including
    *a. Anna Freud
    b. Wilhelm Jung
    c. George Adler
    d. all of the above

19. In Vaillant's system, defense mechanisms are
    a. psychotic
    b. immature
    c. neurotic
    *d. all of the above

20. According to Vaillant, which of the following is a defense mechanism?
    a. humor
    b. altruism
    c. denial
    *d. all of the above

21. A physician who focuses upon his recently deceased mother's tissue biopsy might be using the defense mechanism of
    *a. displacement
    b. distortion
    c. schizoid fantasy
    d. projection

22. As individuals age, they use _____ mature defense mechanisms.
    a. far fewer
    b. fewer
    c. about the same degree of
    *d. a greater proportion of

23. Which of the below is NOT one of the "big five" personality factors?
    a. Neuroticism
    b. Extraversion
    *c. Sensation Seeking
    d. Agreeableness

24. Which personality test is based upon the five-factor model of personality?
    a. 16 PF   c. MMPI-2
    *b. NEO-PI-R   d. CPI

25. The Type-A personality pattern is characterized by
    a. insecurity of status
    b. hyperaggressiveness
    c. sense of time urgency
   *d. all of the above

26. The best way to detect the Type-A personality pattern is
    a. after a coronary
   *b. with a structured interview
    c. with a paper-and-pencil test
    d. none of the above

27. In one study of over 3,000 healthy men, persons with the Type-A personality pattern were _____ to suffer heart attacks than persons with the Type-B pattern.
    a. less likely
    b. no more likely
   *c. 2 1/2 times more likely
    d. 10 times more likely

28. Humanistic, existential, and self theories are all examples of the _____ approach to personality.
    a. modern
   *b. phenomenological
    c. psychoanalytic
    d. none of the above

29. The Q-technique was popularized by
    a. Maddi
   *b. Rogers
    c. Husserl
    d. Bandura

30. A major use of the Q-technique is the study of
    a. unconscious processes
    b. factor-analytic traits
   *c. the self-concept
    d. none of the above

31. In comparing a self-sort with an ideal-sort on the Q-technique, Rogers found that the effects of psychotherapy were to
    a. modify the ideal-sort in a positive direction
    *b. increase congruence between self-sort and ideal-sort
    c. modify the self-sort in a realistic direction
    d. none of the above

32. In general, social learning theorists
    *a. endorse the role of cognitions in behavior
    b. deny that cognitions are helpful in explaining behavior
    c. ignore the effects of cognitions on behavior
    d. none of the above

33. The view that expectations about future outcomes are the primary determinants of behavior was popularized by
    a. Skinner
    b. Bandura
    *c. Rotter
    d. Rogers

34. The Internal-External Scale is a measure of
    a. unconscious thought processes
    b. introversion versus extraversion
    *c. locus of control
    d. all of the above

35. Research indicates that locus of control has a strong relationship to
    a. occupational success
    b. physical health
    c. academic achievement
    *d. all of the above

36. The role of self-efficacy in human action has been popularized by
    a. Skinner
    *b. Bandura
    c. Rotter
    d. Rogers

37. A respected definition of trait is:
   *a. any relatively enduring way in which one individual differs from another
   b. the shared sources of behavior common to persons of similar age
   c. a hypothetical explanation for inconsistencies in the behavior of individuals
   d. none of the above

38. Cattell refers to the more obvious aspects of personality as _____ traits.
   a. source
   *b. surface
   c. persona
   d. cardinal

39. Cattell refers to the stable and constant sources of behavior as _____ traits.
   *a. source
   b. surface
   c. persona
   d. cardinal

40. Cattell identified approximately _____ major traits.
   a. 6
   *b. 16
   c. 60
   d. 100

41. Eysenck's approach to personality is
   a. trait-based
   b. dimensional
   *c. both a and b
   d. neither a nor b

42. According to Mischel, trait scales typically produce validity coefficients with an upper limit of
   *a. .3   c. .7
   b. .5   d. .9

Topic 13B

Projective Techniques

The Projective Hypothesis

A Primer of Projective Techniques

Origins of Projective Techniques
The Popularity of Projective Tests: A Paradox
A Classification of Projective Techniques

Association Techniques

The Rorschach
Comment on the Rorschach
Holtzman Inkblot Technique

Completion Techniques

Sentence Completion Tests
Rotter Incomplete Sentences Blank
Rosenzweig Picture Frustration Study

Construction Techniques

The Thematic Apperception Test (TAT)
The Picture Projective Test
Children's Apperception Test
Other Variations on the TAT

Expression Techniques

The Draw-A-Person Test
The House-Tree-Person Test

Reprise: The Projective Paradox

Case Exhibit 13.1: Projective Tests as Ancillary to the Interview

Summary

Key Terms and Concepts

Classroom Discussion Questions

1. Is the projective hypothesis a tenable one? The instructor might explain the hypothesis and then ask students' opinions. What kinds of evidence would validate the projective hypothesis? Can students cite examples of the apparent validity of the hypothesis?

2. Bring examples of sentence completion stems and responses to class. These could be real examples (borrowed from textbooks on the sentence completion technique) or hypothetical examples. Ask students to speculate about underlying personality characteristics associated with certain kinds of responses.

Extramural Assignments

1. Ask groups of students to devise their own sentence completion test and administer it anonymously to informed volunteers. Then, the students can attempt to score the test according to Rotter's adjustment criteria (discussed in the text). What is the level of interrater agreement for these scores?

2. Require students to read reviews of one or more projective tests from Mental Measurements Yearbook and/or Test Critiques. What is the general tone of the reviews?

Classroom Demonstrations

1. Find an inkblot similar to one of the Rorschach cards and solicit anonymous responses from students. Use the responses to illustrate

aspects of the projective hypothesis, Rorschach scoring, and interpretation.

2. Bring the Family of Man photo essay to class and ask informed volunteers to make up a dramatic story for one or more pictures, including past, present, future, and feelings of the main characters. Engage the class in the "interpretation" of these stories.

Essay Questions

1. What is the projective hypothesis?

2. Describe the manner in which the Rorschach is administered, scored, and interpreted.

3. How can we explain the enduring popularity of projective techniques, given that the psychometric characteristics of these tests are often questionable.

4. Describe the manner in which the Thematic Apperception Test is administered, scored, and interpreted.

5. Compare and contrast the Holtzman Inkblot Technique and the Rorschach.

TEST ITEM FILE

Topic 13B: Projective Techniques

1. Who is generally credited with popularizing the projective hypothesis?
   a. Freud
   b. Jung
   c. Binet
   *d. Frank

2. The idea that personal interpretations of ambiguous stimuli must necessarily reflect the unconscious needs, motives, and conflicts of the examinee is known as the
   a. personality hypothesis
   *b. projective hypothesis
   c. personalogical axiom
   d. psychoanalytic dictum

3. The first projective technique was a(n)
   a. inkblot
   b. story-telling
   *c. word association test
   d. drawing test

4. Administering the Rorschach consists of
   a. free association to inkblots
   b. inquiry about determinants
   *c. both a and b
   d. neither a nor b

5. The Rorschach is scored for
   a. content
   b. determinants
   c. location
   *d. all the above

6. A popular response on the Rorschach is one given by more than _____ percent of the general population.
   a. 10
   *b. 33
   c. 50
   d. 67

7. Most experts agree that the preferred method for scoring the Rorschach is the one developed by
   a. Klopfer
   b. Hertz
   c. Beck
   *d. Exner

8. On the Rorschach, the F+% is
    a. the frequency of total responses for all ten inkblots
    b. the frequency of popular responses for all ten inkblots
    *c. the proportion of the total responses which use pure form as a determinant
    d. none of the above

9. On the Rorschach, when the F+% falls below 70%, the examiner should consider the possibility of
    a. severe psychopathology
    b. organicity
    c. intellectual deficit
    *d. all of the above

10. The purpose of the Rorschach is to
    a. derive a psychiatric diagnosis
    b. estimate prognosis for psychotherapy
    c. formulate complex personality structures
    *d. all of the above

11. In one prominent Rorschach study, expert judges rated _____ percent of normal persons to be psychotic.
    a. 4
    *b. 24
    c. 44
    d. 64

12. The Holtzman Inkblot Test (HIT) differs from the Rorschach in the following way(s):
    a. only one response is allowed per HIT card
    b. the HIT comes in two parallel forms
    *c. both a and b
    d. neither a nor b

13. For most categories, interscorer agreement on the Holtzman Inkblot Test is on the order of
    a. .65   c. .85
    b. .75   *d. .95

14. On word association tests, blocking or the inability to offer a response is thought to be indicative of
    a. depression
   *b. schizophrenia
    c. alcoholism
    d. none of the above

15. The most widely used sentence completion test is the
   *a. Rotter Incomplete Sentences Blank
    b. Washington University Sentence Completion Test
    c. Bloom Sentence Completion Survey
    d. Incomplete Sentences Task

16. Scoring on the Rotter Incomplete Sentences Blank consists of
    a. six different dimensions rated 1 to 9
   *b. a single maladjustment score
    c. both a and b
    d. neither a nor b

17. The Rosenzweig Picture Frustration Study is scored for
    a. extragression
    b. intragression
   *c. both a and b
    d. neither a nor b

18. The textbook takes the position that the Rosenzweig Picture Frustration Study is suited to
   *a. research
    b. individual assessment
    c. both a and b
    d. neither a nor b

19. In administering the TAT, the examiner requests the examinee to
    a. make up a dramatic story for each picture
    b. tell what led up to the current scene
    c. describe how the characters are thinking and feeling
   *d. all of the above

20. The TAT was originally designed to assess
    a. needs
    b. press
    *c. both a and b
    d. neither a nor b

21. The TAT is best regarded as a(n)
    a. test
    *b. method
    c. interview
    d. none of the above

22. In most cases, interpretation of the TAT is based upon
    a. quantitative scoring
    *b. the hero assumption
    c. comparison to sample stories
    d. none of the above

23. Stimuli for the Picture Projective Test are based upon
    a. actual photographs taken by the test authors
    *b. the Family of Man photo album
    c. a collection of optimistic photographs from Life magazine
    d. none of the above

24. Formal scoring for the Children's Apperception Test is
    a. based upon responses for 1,000 normal children
    b. guided by a careful manual
    *c. nonexistent
    d. none of the above

25. The Children's Apperception Test is designed to assess
    a. conflicts   c. defenses
    b. anxieties   *d. all of the above

26. Which test is designed expressly for Hispanic persons?
    a. T-TAT
    *b. TEMAS
    c. H-TAT
    d. none of the above

27. Interpretation of the Draw-A-Person test is
    a. quantitative
    *b. clinical-intuitive
    c. both a and b
    d. neither a nor b

28. In the House-Tree-Person test, the drawing of the tree is thought to mirror the subject's
    a. intrafamilial relationships
    *b. environmental experiences
    c. interpersonal relationships
    d. none of the above

29. Regarding validational research, the author of the House-Tree-Person test asserts
    a. the evidence is weakly supportive of the test's validity
    b. the evidence is stronly supportive of the test's validity
    *c. validational research is not possible with this test
    d. none of the above

30. The textbook takes the position that figure-drawing approaches to the assessment of personality
    *a. have no proven validity
    b. are valid in selected instances
    c. are valid in the majority of cases
    d. are valid when quantitative scoring systems are used

31. According to the textbook, the continuing popularity of projective methods can be traced to the fact that
    a. these methods have strong validity in the hands of experienced examiners
    b. test publishers have a vested interest in promoting their instruments
    *c. clinicians notice only the confirming instances
    d. none of the above

32. The fact that clinicians notice the confirming instances, but ignore the more numerous findings which contradict expectations is referred to as
    *a. illusory validation
    b. selective perception
    c. confirmatory bias
    d. none of the above

Topic 14A

Self-Report Inventories

Theory-Guided Inventories

 Edwards Personal Preference Schedule
 Personality Research Form
 Myers-Briggs Type Indicator (MBTI)
 Measures of Type A Behavior
 State-Trait Anxiety Inventory (STAI)

Factor-Analytically Derived Inventories

 Sixteen Personality Factor Questionnaire (16 PF)
 Eysenck Personality Questionnaire
 Comrey Personality Scales
 NEO Personality Inventory-Revised

Criterion-Keyed Inventories

 Minnesota Multiphasic Personality Inventory (MMPI)
  and MMPI-2
 MMPI-2 Interpretation
 Technical Properties of the MMPI-2
 Minnesota Multiphasic Personality Inventory-2 (MMPI-2)
 California Psychological Inventory (CPI)
 Millon Clinical Multiaxial Inventory-II (MCMI-II)
 Personality Inventory for Children (PIC)

Summary

Key Terms and Concepts

Classroom Discussion Questions

1. Compare and contrast the Edwards Personal Preference Schedule (EPPS) and the Personality Research Form (PRF).

2. What are the advantages and disadvantages of different scale construction techniques? Ask students to compare and contrast criterion-keyed, rational, and factor analytic methods.

3. Regarding the Personality Inventory for Children (PIC), is it reasonable to assume that parents are good informants about their children?

Extramural Assignments

1. The following general assignment can be given for any or all of the tests discussed in this chapter: find research articles which use the test in question; then, summarize the findings. How was the test used? What bearing do the results have upon the apparent validity of the test?

Classroom Demonstrations

1. Invite a counselor or therapist to class to discuss the value of personality testing in his/her work. Which tests do they use? Why?

2. The relationship between test profiles and personality interpretation can be displayed for most of the instruments discussed in this topic. For example, the instructor might seek out books on the MMPI-2 which portray average profiles for different diagnostic categories. The profiles can be displayed on overhead transparency and the corresponding personality interpretations can be discussed.

Essay Questions

1. Discuss the format used by the Edwards Personal Preference Schedule. What is the current standing of this test in the professional community?

2. Describe the Myers-Briggs Type Indicator and discuss the dimensions of personality tested by this instrument.

3. Compare and contrast the Jenkins Activity Survey and the Survey of Work Styles. What is the purpose of these instruments? How well do they fulfill that purpose?

4. Describe the 16 PF and discuss how it was constructed.

5. Describe and discuss the dimensions of personality measured by the Eysenck Personality Questionnaire.

6. Describe the validity scales from the MMPI-2. Also, list at least seven of the ten clinical scales.

7. Compare and contrast the MMPI-2 and the CPI.

TEST ITEM FILE

Topic 14A: Self-Report Inventories

1. The Woodworth Personal Data Sheet was designed for mass screening of military recruits during
   *a. World War I
   b. World War II
   c. Korean War
   d. Vietnam War

2. The content of the Personal Data Sheet was based upon
   a. complaints of 1,000 inductees
   b. items nominated by a panel of psychologists
   *c. a structured psychiatric interview
   d. none of the above

3. The Edwards Personal Preference Scale was an attempt to measure
   a. Jungian personality types
   b. Freudian personality structures
   *c. needs of Henry Murray
   d. none of the above

4. The Edwards Personal Preference Scale consists of _____ items.
   a. true-false
   b. like-indifferent-dislike
   *c. forced-choice
   d. none of the above

5. The format of the Edwards Personal Preference Scale was designed to deal with the problem of
   a. excessive test length
   b. scale overlap
   *c. social desirability
   d. none of the above

6. Scale scores on the Edwards Personal Preference Scale are designed to be
    a. normative
    *b. ipsative
    c. criterion-related
    d. none of the above

7. The Personality Research Form was designed to measure
    a. Jungian personality types
    b. Freudian personality structures
    *c. needs of Henry Murray
    d. none of the above

8. Scale items for the Personality Research Form were selected on the basis of
    a. high biserial correlations with total scale scores
    b. low correlation with scores on the other scales
    *c. both a and b
    d. neither a nor b

9. The Myers-Briggs Type Indicator was designed to assess
    *a. Jungian personality types
    b. Freudian personality structures
    c. needs of Henry Murray
    d. none of the above

10. The Myers-Briggs Type Indicator is scored on
    a. Extraversion-Introversion
    b. Thinking-Feeling
    c. Judging-Perceptive
    *d. all of the above

11. Which of the following is NOT a subscale of the Jenkins Activity Survey?
    a. Speed and Impatient
    b. Job Involvement
    c. Hard-driving and Competitive
    *d. Anger Management

12. The Survey of Work Styles is an index of
    a. vocational needs
    b. work styles
    *c. Type A behavior
    d. none of the above

13. The transitory feelings of fear or worry which most of us experience on occasion:
    *a. state anxiety
    b. trait anxiety
    c. free-floating anxiety
    d. neurotic anxiety

14. The relatively stable tendency of an individual to respond anxiously to a stressful predicament:
    a. state anxiety
    *b. trait anxiety
    c. free-floating anxiety
    d. neurotic anxiety

15. The 16 PF yields a total of _____ indices or attributes of personality.
    a. 16
    *b. 20
    c. 32
    d. 64

16. Studies with the 16 PF indicate that stably married couples are _____ unstably married couples.
    a. less alike than
    *b. more alike than
    c. complementary opposites in comparison to
    d. none of the above

17. The Eysenck Personality Questionnaire is designed to measure
    a. Psychoticism
    b. Extraversion
    c. Neuroticism
    *d. all of the above

18. According to Eysenck, introverts
    a. are more vigilant in watchkeeping
    b. do better at signal-detection tasks
    c. are less tolerant of pain
   *d. all of the above

19. This test is based upon the five-factor model of personality.
    a. MMPI-2
    b. MCMI-II
   *c. NEO PI-R
    d. none of the above

20. The Comrey Personality Scales were developed with
   *a. college students
    b. general adults
    c. both a and b
    d. neither a nor b

21. In a _____ approach, test items are assigned to a particular scale if, and only if, they discriminate between a well-defined criterion group and a relevant control group.
   *a. criterion-keyed
    b. rationally-keyed
    c. normative
    d. none of the above

22. Suppose a test developer using the criterion-keyed approach finds that the item "I like to read technical blueprints" (answered false) is assigned to the depression scale. What should the test developer do?
    a. search for a theoretical link between depression and blueprint reading
    b. discard the item because most likely it is an anomalous happening
   *c. keep the item on the scale
    d. none of the above

23. The items on the MMPI-2 encompass
    a. anxieties and phobias
    b. depressive and manic symptoms
    c. neurologic symptoms
    *d. all of the above

24. The MMPI-2 incorporates the following validity scale(s):
    a. Cannot Say
    b. Lie
    c. Frequency
    *d. all of the above

25. Which MMPI-2 scale was designed to detect a subtle form of defensiveness?
    a. L or Lie
    b. F or Frequency
    *c. K or Correction
    d. ? or Cannot Say

26. On the MMPI-2, portions of the K-scale score are added to
    a. experimental scales only
    *b. some of the regular clinical scales
    c. all of the regular clinical scales
    d. all of the scales, regular and experimental

27. A major criticism of the MMPI-2 is that
    a. test-retest correlations are very low
    *b. intercorrelations among the clinical scales are very high
    c. normal persons commonly produce abnormal test profiles
    d. scale interpretations are based upon inadequate research

28. The California Psychological Inventory was designed to
    a. measure the dimensions of normal personality
    b. reflect "folk" concepts of personality
    *c. both a and b
    d. neither a nor b

29. The CPI has been proved useful in the prediction of
    a. college achievement
    b. executive success
    c. effectiveness of law officers
    *d. all of the above

30. Which test is planned and organized to identify clinical patterns in a manner that is compatible with the Diagnostic and Statistical Manual (DSM-IV) of the American Psychiatric Association?
    a. Minnesota Multiphasic Personality Inventory-2
    *b. Millon Clinical Multiaxial Inventory-II
    c. California Psychological Inventory
    d. none of the above

31. Which test is better suited to the diagnosis of acute clinical syndromes?
    *a. Minnesota Multiphasic Personality Inventory-2
    b. Millon Clinical Multiaxial Inventory-II
    c. California Psychological Inventory
    d. none of the above

32. In the Personality Inventory for Children, responses consist of
    a. true-false answers from the children
    b. like-indifferent-dislike answers from the children
    *c. true-false answers from parents or caretakers
    d. like-indifferent-dislike answers from caretakers

33. In a mixed sample of clinical and nonclinical children, the Personality Inventory for Children is about ____ percent accurate in classifying children as needing or not needing special services.
    a. 60
    b. 70
    c. 80
    *d. 90

34. The NEO PI-R assesses all of the following EXCEPT
    *a. sensation-seeking   c. openness to experience
    b. agreeableness   d. neuroticism

Topic 14B

Behavioral Assessment and Related Approaches

Foundations of Behavior Therapy

Behavior Therapy and Behavioral Assessment

Exposure-Based Methods
Contingency Management Procedures
Cognitive Behavior Therapies
Self-Monitoring Procedures

Assessment of Nonverbal Behavior

Visual Interaction
Paralinguistics
Facial Expression

Profile of Nonverbal Sensitivity (PONS)

Summary

Key Terms and Concepts

Classroom Discussion Questions

1. What are the fundamental assumptions of behavioral assessment? How does it differ from more traditional approaches to assessment?

2. For the major approaches to behavioral therapy (exposure-based methods, contingency management, cognitive behavior therapy, self-monitoring) what are some typical approaches to assessment?

3. What are some examples of nonverbal behavior? Ask students to describe real-life examples of the nonverbal behavior of friends or acquaintances.

Extramural Assignments

1. Request that students read about examples of token economies in clinical journals. For specific applications of the token economy method, what are the difficulties inherent to this approach? How is progress gauged?

2. Ask students to read articles from behaviorally oriented journals such as Journal of Applied Behavior Analysis. What kinds of assessment approaches are used in this field?

3. Using themselves as research subjects, students can implement a version of Lewinsohn's Pleasant Events Schedule. Is there a positive relationship between engaging in pleasant events and improved mood?

Classroom Demonstrations

1. The difficulties of rating nonverbal behavior can be demonstrated through role playing exercises. Invite student actors and actresses to class to depict various emotions in an nonverbal manner. Ask students to determine which emotions are being depicted.

2. Invite a behaviorally oriented psychologist to class as a guest speaker. Ask this resource person to discuss two issues: what is the value of traditional personality tests? And, what assessment approaches does this person use in his/her clinical work?

Essay Questions

1. What are the fundamental assumptions of behavioral assessment?

2. Compare and contrast behavioral assessment with more traditional forms of personality assessment.

3. Describe the Profile of Nonverbal Sensitivity. Discuss reliability and validity findings.

4. What is the Facial Action Coding System?

5. Describe the nature and purpose of the Pleasant Events Schedule.

6. What is the relationship between behavior therapy and behavioral assessment?

TEST ITEM FILE

Topic 14B: Behavioral Assessment and Related Approaches

1. One important difference between behavioral assessment and traditional assessment is that the former is
  *a. more directly tied to treatment
  b. more complex
  c. less respected by clinicians
  d. none of the above

2. Behavior therapy is also called
  a. insight therapy
  *b. behavior modification
  c. consequence therapy
  d. none of the above

3. Wolpe's work emphasized
  a. systematic treatment of phobias
  b. animal models of human problems
  *c. both a and b
  d. neither a nor b

4. Bandura emphasized the role of _____ in the behavioral approach.
  a. punishment
  b. authority figures
  *c. observational learning
  d. none of the above

5. In a behavioral avoidance test (BAT), the therapist assesses
   a. the client's stated level of fear of a situation
   *b. how long the client can tolerate the feared stimulus
   c. the strategies by which the client avoids a feared stimulus
   d. none of the above

6. Fear survey schedules are often used to
   a. screen large samples of persons
   b. monitor changes in fears
   *c. both a and b
   d. neither a nor b

7. Token economies possess the following limitation(s):
   a. poor generalization of the target behaviors beyond the
treatment program
   b. difficulties in training staff to properly implement token
economies
   c. client resistance to participation
   *d. all of the above

8. According to Beck, depression consists of
   a. a pessimistic view of the world
   b. a pessimistic self-concept
   c. a pessimistic view of the future
   *d. all of the above

9. According to research findings, the most effective way to teach
assertiveness is
   a. self-help manual
   b. therapist instructions
   *c. role playing
   d. none of the above

10. The Pleasant Events Schedule monitors
   a. frequency of daily events
   b. pleasantness of daily events
   *c. both a and b
   d. neither a nor b

11. In the Pleasant Events Schedule, the mean rate of pleasant events is calculated by
    a. summing frequency of events
    b. summing pleasantness of events
    *c. summing frequency x pleasantness of events
    d. none of the above

12. Which of the following is a paralinguistic cue?
    a. facial expression
    b. bodily movement
    *c. tone of voice
    d. none of the above

13. According to research on gaze, dishonest persons _____ visual interaction during episodes of deception.
    *a. reduce
    b. maintain the same level of
    c. increase
    d. maintain complete

14. According to the textbook, what are the prospects for the development of standardized tests for the assessment of gaze and mutual gaze?
    a. excellent
    b. fair
    c. very difficult but possible
    *d. essentially impossible

15. The purpose of passing a person's voice through a low-pass filter to remove high-frequency sounds is to
    a. enhance emotional aspects
    b. diminish emotional nuances
    *c. filter out the content
    d. none of the above

16. In one study, the correlation between doctor's underlying anger and their effectiveness in referring alcoholics was
    a. .33   c. -.33
    b. .66   *d. -.66

17. According to Ekman and Friesen, all facial movement can be traced to ___ facial action units.
    a. 10
    b. 22
    *c. 44
    d. 110

18. The validity of the Facial Action Coding System (FACS) is
    a. unknown
    b. poor
    *c. well established
    d. irrelevant--this is not a test

19. When the experimenter unintentionally influences subjects to change their behavior in the direction of the experimenter's expectations, this is known as
    a. subject bias effect
    b. Heisenberg's hypothesis
    *c. experimenter expectancy effect
    d. subjective collusion

20. The stimuli for the Profile of Nonverbal Sensitivity are administered
    a. orally   *c. by film
    b. by questionnaire   d. none of the above

21. Test-retest reliability for the individual channels of the PONS is typically in the
    *a. .20s and .30s
    b. .40s and .50s
    c. .60s and .70s
    d. .80s and .90s

22. The correlation between PONS scores and IQ scores is
    a. unknown
    *b. low and positive
    c. high and positive
    d. moderate and negative

23. What does the Automatic Thoughts Questionnaire measure?
    *a. frequency of depression-related cognitions
    b. depth of obsessive ruminations
    c. distress level of phobic objects
    d. none of the above

24. A serious problem with fear survey schedules is
    *a. they may lack validity
    b. that most of them are too long
    c. the instructions are occasionally misunderstood
    d. all of the above

25. The purpose of the Body Image Testng System is to assess
    a. perceptual distortions
    b. actual self-image
    c. ideal self-image
    *d. all of the above

Topic 15A:

Computer-Assisted Psychological Assessment

Computers in Testing: Overview and History

    Brief History of CAPA

Computer-Based Test Interpretation: Current Status

    Scoring Reports
    Descriptive Reports
    Actuarial Reports: Clnical vs. Actuarial Prediction
    Actuarial Interpretation: Sample Approach
    Computer-Assisted Clinical Reports

Multimedia: The New Horizon of CAPA

Evaluation of Computer-Based Test Interpretation

    Advantages of Computerized Testing and Report Writing

    Disadvantages of Computerized Testing and Report Writing

Computerized Adaptive Testing

Summary

Key Terms and Concepts

Classroom Discussion Questions

1. What are the advantages and pitfalls of computerized testing and report writing? Perhaps some of the students have had experiences with computerized narrative reports. What were their experiences?

2. What is the distinction between the clinical and the actuarial method? Which is generally superior?

Extramural Assignments

1. Request students to read back issues of the APA Monitor to determine the extent to which psychological tests and report writing are now available in computerized format. Which tests can be submitted for computerized narrative reports? What do we know about the sources of those reports?

Classroom Demonstrations

1. Bring examples of computerized test interpretations to class. With advanced preparation, the instructor can usually obtain sample reports for free by writing companies that advertise in the APA Monitor.

Essay Questions

1. What are some of the ethical and legal problems raised by the practice of computerizing narrative reports for psychological tests?

2. Distinguish actuarial from clinical prediction. In general, which is superior?

3. Describe computerized adaptive testing.

TEST ITEM FILE

Topic 15A: Computer-Aided Psychological Assessment

1. The computer has been used in testing for
    a. presenting test instructions
    b. administering stimuli or questions
    c. tailoring item difficulty levels to the examinee
    *d. all of the above

2. The use of computers to provide test *interpretations* can be traced to
    *a. the Mayo Clinic in the early 1960s
    b. the Strong Vocational Interest Blank in the 1920s
    c. the MMPI in the late 1940s
    d. none of the above

3. The first automation of the entire psychological assessment process occurred at the
    a. NIMH in Washington, DC
    b. Mayo Clinic in Minnesota
    *c. Salt Lake City VA Hospital
    d. U.S. Army Headquarters, Quantico, VA

4. Multimedia computerized testing has been used for
    *a. assessment of applicants for manufacturing jobs
    b. assessment of applicants for police jobs
    c. both a and b
    d. neither a nor b

5. In the actuarial method _____ formula is used to diagnose or predict behavior.
    *a. an empirically derived
    b. a clinically derived
    c. any reasonable
    d. none of the above

6. How do clinical and actuarial prediction compare?
   a. clinical is almost always superior
   b. clinical is usually superior
   c. actuarial is usually superior
   *d. actuarial is almost always superior

7. In computerized adaptive testing, testing continues until
   a. the examinee fails a specific number of items in a row
   *b. a predetermined level of measurement accuracy is achieved
   c. the examinee is administered the most difficult item
   d. none of the above

8. The practice of computerized report writing raises the following concern(s)
   a. computerized narrative reports are rarely validated prior to use
   b. computerized clinical psychological interpretations are unsigned
   *c. both a and b
   d. neither a nor b

9. What is the position of the American Psychological Association with respect to computerized testing?
   a. the organization takes no position
   b. the organization gives unqualified endorsement
   *c. the organization publishes guidelines for computerized reports
   d. none of the above

10. Regarding cost, research on the utility of computerized testing indicates that the cost is
    a. only slightly lower than traditional approaches
    b. more expensive but reports are more accurate
    *c. about half that of traditional approaches
    d. about one-tenth that of traditional approaches

11. Compared to traditional testing, computerized adaptive testing provides extreme scores which are
    a. less accurate
    *b. more accurate
    c. equally accurate
    d. regressed more toward the mean

12. On average, computerized adaptive testing reduces testing time by about _____ percent.
    a. 25
    *b. 50
    c. 75
    d. 90

13. Currently, computerized adaptive testing is used by
    a. large school systems
    b. inpatient psychiatric wards
    *c. U.S. Army
    d. all of the above

14. One test that makes use of actuarial interpretation is
    *a. Personality Inventory for Children
    b. Millon MCMI-II
    c. Wechsler Adult Intelligence Scale-Revised
    d. all of the above

15. For which of the following is a computerized narrative report available?
    a. 16 PF
    b. MMPI-2
    c. CPI
    *d. all of the above

Topic 15B

Professional Standards, Ethical Issues, and Courtroom Testimony

Ethical and Professional Standards in Testing

    Best Interests of the Client
    Confidentiality and the Duty to Warn
    Expertise of the Test User
    Informed Consent
    Consideration of Individual Differences
    Obsolete Tests and the Standard of Care

Case Exhibit 15.2: Overzealous Interpretation of the MMPI

Psychological Tests and Courtroom Testimony

    Standards For the Expert Witness
    Not Guilty By Reason of Insanity
    Competency to Stand Trial
    The Prediction of Violence
    Child Custody
    Personal Injury and Related Testimony
    Interpretation of Polygraph Records

Controversy Over the Psychologist as Expert Witness

Reprise: Responsible Test Use

Summary

Key Terms and Concepts

Classroom Discussion Questions

1. Discuss each of the broad ethical principles that apply to testing, asking students to cite hypothetical examples where these principles might be violated. The principles are: assessment should be in the best interests of the client; practitioners have a primary obligation to protect the confidentiality of test results; the psychologist must possess the expertise needed to evaluate the tests that are chosen for an assessment, the test user must obtain informed consent from the test taker or a legal representative; the examiner must be knowledgeable about individual differences; and, the psychologist must respect the current standards of care.

2. How do students feel about the insanity defense? Do they really understand the conditions of the defense?

3. Ask students to compare and contrast the M'Naughten rule and the Model Penal Code. Which is a better code? Are there cases where one code would apply, but the other wouldn't?

4. Ask students to compare and contrast the insanity defense with the issue of competency to stand trial. Are these concepts synonymous?

5. How well can psychologists predict future violence? Ask students to speculate upon why it is so difficult to make accurate predictions of whether a defendant will be violent in the future.

Extramural Assignments

1. Have students read the Ethical Principles of Psychologists (found in the December, 1992 issue of the American Psychologist) and summarize the main points.

2. Urge students to attend open court for trials that involve psychological testimony. What was the testimony of the psychologist? What tests, if any, did he/she rely upon for the testimony? How was the expertise of the psychologist established?

3. Require students to visit a law library and look up books, journals, and articles that pertain to the interface between law and psychology.

Classroom Demonstrations

1. Invite a forensic or consulting psychologist to class to discuss his/her experiences in court.

2. Bring a copy of the Ethical Principles of Psychologists to class and discuss specific principles.

4. Invite a lawyer to class to discuss the role of psychologists and psychological tests in the courtroom.

Essay Questions

1. Discuss the major ethical principles that govern the practice of psychology, including the practice of psychological testing.

2. Discuss the insanity defense, providing definitions of prevailing laws. Is the defense respected by experts in jurisprudence?

3. Describe the Rogers Criminal Responsibility Scales.

4. What are some of the problems encountered in the prediction of violent behavior?

5. Discuss the role of the expert witness in psychology. What is an expert witness? What is the view of the skeptics on this issue?

TEST ITEM FILE

Topic 15B: Professional Standards, Ethical Issues, and Courtroom Testimony

1. The single most important principle in the ethics of testing is
   a. confidentiality
   b. informed consent
   *c. best interests of the client
   d. validity of results

2. With respect to the confidentiality of test results
   a. there are no exceptions
   b. exceptions can be made if law enforcement officers make an official request
   *c. exceptions can be made only if withholding information would present a clear danger to client or others
   d. exceptions can be made if clergy make an official request

3. According to the principle of _____ test takers or representatives are made aware, in language that they can understand, of the reasons for testing, the type of tests to be used, the intended use and the range of material consequences of the intended use.
   a. confidentiality
   *b. informed consent
   c. best interests of the client
   d. validity of results

4. According to the 1923 court case Frye v. United States, an expert witness
   a. can present testimony based upon any procedures he or she desires
   b. can offer expert opinions based upon only his judgment
   *c. should use well-established and accepted tests and procedures
   d. none of the above

5. In general, what is the view of legal experts on the insanity plea?
    a. the majority favor its abolishment
    b. most would like to see it restricted further
    *c. the insanity plea is widely respected by legal experts
    d. none of the above

6. According to the _____, it must be clearly proved that, at the time of the committing of the act, the party accused was laboring under such a defect of reason, from disease of the mind, as not to know the nature and quality of the act he was doing.
    *a. M'Naughten rule
    b. Model Penal Code rule
    c. Durham rule
    d. none of the above

7. According to the _____, a person is not responsible for criminal conduct if at the time of such conduct, as a result of mental disease or defect, he lacks substantial capacity either to appreciate the criminality [wrongfulness] of his conduct or to conform his conduct to the requirements of the law.
    a. M'Naughten rule
    *b. Model Penal Code rule
    c. Durham rule
    d. none of the above

8. The Model Penal Code rule contains provisions which prohibit the inclusion of the _____ within the insanity defense.
    a. mentally retarded
    b. multiple personality
    *c. antisocial personality
    d. all of the above

9. The Rogers Criminal Responsibility Assessment Scales consist of
    a. true-false items
    *b. a series of rating scales filled out by the examiner
    c. a series of rating scales filled out by the criminal
    d. none of the above

10. Competency to stand trial is assessed by a defendant's ability to
    a. understand the proceedings   *c. both a and b
    b. assist in his defense   d. neither a nor b

11. Incompetency to stand trial and legal insanity are
    a. synonymous
    b. synonymous in the majority of cases
   *c. separate and distinct concepts
    d. related in that legal insanity implies incompetency

12. A major practical problem for researchers attempting to predict violent behavior is
    a. the definition of violence is vague
   *b. violence occurs with very low frequency in the general population
    c. the causes of violence are unknown
    d. none of the above

13. For persons with a violent history, a probability of imminent violence can be derived from
    a. the number of previous serious acts of violence
    b. substance abuse within the previous month
    c. actual or threatened breakup of love relationship
   *d. all of the above

14. What is the role of psychological testing in helping to determine child custody?
    a. tests are not allowed in most jurisdictions
   *b. tests results are rarely helpful in making custody decisions
    c. test results can be decisive in awarding custody
    d. none of the above

15. In the classic Goldberg study on diagnostic accuracy of brain damage from Bender Gestalt drawings, which of the below is the correct rank ordering for group accuracy?
   *a. graduate students, office staff, Ph.D. psychologists
    b. office staff, graduate students, Ph.D. psychologists
    c. Ph.D. psychologists, graduate students, office staff
    d. Ph.D. psychologists, office staff, graduate students

16. The Employee Polygraph Protection Act
    a. specifies that employees must be forewarned as to the scope of a polygraph examination
    b. specifies that employers must obtain the explicit informed consent of employees before giving a polygraph examination
    *c. prohibits private employers from requesting or requiring pre-employment polygraph examinations
    d. none of the above

17. A polygraph detects
    *a. physiological arousal
    b. the act of lying
    c. both a and b
    d. neither a nor b

18. In field studies of polygrapher accuracy, the most common error is
    *a. innocent persons proclaimed guilty
    b. guilty persons proclaimed innocent
    c. both a and b
    d. unknown--relevant field studies do not exist